THE LIBRARY
ST. MARY'S COLLEGE OF MARYLAND
ST. MARY'S CITY, MARYLAND 20686

The World Energy Triangle

A Strategy for Cooperation

The World Energy Triangle

A Strategy
for Cooperation

Thomas Hoffmann
Brian Johnson

International Institute for Environment and Development

Ballinger Publishing Company ● Cambridge, Massachusetts
A Subsidiary of Harper & Row, Publishers, Inc.

Copyright © 1981 by International Institute for Environment and Development. All rights reserved. No part of this publication may be reproduced, stored in a retrieval system, or transmitted in any form or by any means, electronic, mechanical, photocopy, recording or otherwise, without the prior written consent of the publisher.

International Standard Book Number: 0-905347-15-3

Library of Congress Catalog Card Number: 80-18952

Printed in the United States of America

Library of Congress Cataloging in Publication Data

Hoffmann, Thomas.
  World energy triangle.

  Bibliography: p.
  Includes index.
  1. Underdeveloped areas—Energy policy. 2. Energy
policy. I. Johnson, Brian D. G., joint author.
II. Title.
HD9502.A2H633   333.79'09172'4   80-18952
ISBN 0-905347-15-3

Contents

Foreword

It is becoming widely believed that the world energy crisis could be the progenitor of a new era of economic opportunity. This book offers support to that belief. It comes at a time when the dialogue between Northern "haves" and Southern "have nots" (particularly those who have no oil) has been frozen by fear and suspicion. At such a time, the only hope is to focus on potential areas of common interest and practical cooperation. My colleagues argue in this book that the best opportunity for bold initiatives in the international community, from which everyone could profit, is the development of new sources of energy supply, particularly in the oil-poor countries of the South. These sources should be able to use these countries' natural advantages—above all direct energy from the sun—in ways that will help to solve their central problem of rural poverty.

What gives this theme its particular interest is the growing recognition in the industrial North that by early in the next century their own economic destiny will hang increasingly on success in adapting renewable energy sources. This applies equally to the present oil exporters of OPEC, whose interest in examining and investing in the great energy transition is documented here.

This volume serves the important purpose of documenting the progress—and the suspicions, misunderstandings, and institutional bottlenecks—that have shaped cooperation and conflict over energy between the West, the oil-rich states, and the poor, oil-importing developing countries. The authors see these three groups locked in a triangle of suspicion that could, however, become a triangle of cooperation to everyone's advantage.

In addressing themselves to "A Strategy for Cooperation," the authors discuss not only the politics in energy cooperation and the characteristics of energy sources in relation to the objectives that they are supposed to meet, but also present and prospective policies for energy production. They concentrate particularly on solar energy—discussing the prospects for mutually profitable transactions between suppliers and recipients and the mediating role the governments can and should play in this rapidly growing market.

A feature of this volume that I believe gives it particular relevance and importance is the authors' insistence on seeing energy production, and the economic and social development it is supposed to secure, in the total context of the physical environment. To the technologically minded, discussions of the importance of fuelwood programs to soil conservation and climate may seem remote from the price of a kilowatt hour of hydro-electricity, or of a joule of energy caught from a methane digester. But Hoffmann and Johnson illustrate why they are intimately connected, and why it is vital that we bridge these conceptual divides and see energy production and use "in the round" as an inseparable part of the task of managing and conserving the environment.

Both for its conceptual breadth and its practical suggestions for modest, realistic steps toward negotiated programs for energy cooperation, this book should provide a "lamp unto the weary feet" of the whole development community—whether to the official, academic, or business concerns at each corner of the "suspicious triangle." I commend it to them all.

William Clark
President
International Institute for
Environment and Development

Acknowledgments

This book was made possible by a supporting grant to the International Institute for Environment and Development from the ARCO Foundation, and our thanks are due to them for their generous help.

We would also like to thank the more than one hundred officials of aid agencies, government ministries, and international organizations whose policies and programs were the target of our research. They were generous in the time they gave to discuss the issues presented here.

As authors it has been our aim to avoid the inherent and unnoticed Western bias of most writers on oil and energy issues. Inevitably, however, while we have sought detachment, we cannot claim an Olympian view. We are aware, for example, that an author from an OPEC country with a similar commitment to balance would have written a quite different book.

We owe a great debt of gratitude to IIED staff who contributed a large amount of background research and assistance: Christine Glenday, who particularly contributed to Chapter 3; Ariane van Buren, who researched French policy and programs; Mike Whiteman, Joe Chapel, and Edda Post, who compiled the statistical tables. Our particular gratitude goes to Todd Bartlem who not only researched Chapter 4 but also solved every problem, large and small, that reached his desk. We wish also to thank Shelley Dobyns, Virpi

Kairinen, Catherine Nesbet, and Nancy Shepherd for their cheerful energy in preparing successive drafts of the manuscript.

More than thirty individuals read an early draft. We appreciate the comments and advice of them all, but wish particularly to thank Barbara Ward Jackson and Abdlatif Y. Al-Hamad, as well as Robert Blake, Gillian Brown, Erik Eckholm, Efrain Friedmann, William Knowland, David Runnalls, David Satterthwaite, and Gregory Thomas. However, the judgments made and any errors of fact or interpretation are of course the responsibility of the authors alone.

Finally, energy politics and finance are, at the time of publication, so volatile, that we have avoided discussion of the twists and turns of immediate issues. We cannot help recalling H.L. Mencken's telegram to the *Baltimore Sun* during the 1924 Democratic Convention. During this, the longest Convention in American political history, Mencken telegraphed, as a lead to Baltimore, "Only one thing is certain after the 101st ballot of this Convention. John W. Davies will never be nominated". Following Davies' nomination on the 103rd ballot, Mencken cabled "I hope some idiot will have the sense to remove the negative." We will not be in a position to send such a message to our longsuffering publishers.

Thomas Hoffmann
Brian Johnson

September 1980

List of Figures and Tables

List of Acronyms

ACP	Atlantic, Caribbean, Pacific states (parties to the Lomé Convention, with the members of the European Economic Community)
ADB	Asian Development Bank
AID	Agency for International Development (United States)
BMZ	Bundesministerium für Wirtschaftliche Zusammenarbeit (Federal Republic of Germany)
CEA	Commissariat à l'Énergie Atomique (French Atomic Energy Commission)
CIEC	Conference on International Economic Cooperation
COMES	Commissariat à l'Énergie Solaire (France)
DAC	Development Assistance Committee (of the OECD)
DOE	Department of Energy (United States)
EDF	European Development Fund
EEC	European Economic Community (Common Market)
FAC	Fonds d'Assistance et de Coordination (France)
IAEA	International Atomic Energy Agency
IBRD	International Bank for Reconstruction and Development (World Bank)
IDB	Inter-American Development Bank
IEA	International Energy Agency
LDC	Less Developed Country
NIEO	New International Economic Order
ODA	Official Development Assistance
OECD	Organization for Economic Cooperation and Development

OIDC	Oil Importing Developing Countries
OLADE	Latin American Regional Energy Organization
OPEC	Organization of Petroleum Exporting Countries
U.K.ODA	Overseas Development Administration (United Kingdom)
UNCTAD	United Nations Conference on Trade and Development
UNDP	United Nations Development Programme
UNIDO	United Nations Industrial Development Organization
VIF	Venezuelan Investment Fund

Introduction

War may be man's oldest pastime, but energy is his newest
obsession. Worldwide public attention has fixed on energy
probably more than on any other peacetime issue in recent
memory. The contortions of nations and international institutions to
meet the challenge of OPEC have dominated cabinets, Great Power
summits, the North-South dialogue, and deliberations of the United
Nations. Scarcely a day passes without some new variation on the
political threats to energy supply or the announcement of an exciting
alternative energy prospect. Recent political and military events,
moreover, have deepened concern that the stakes in the contest for
oil and its influence have become so high that regional, and perhaps
world, peace will be threatened in the 1980s.

With Western lifestyles facing severe modification, and with Middle Eastern stability apparently threatened by the clash between
modernization and fundamentalism, it is hardly surprising that the
continuously worsening energy plight of the poor countries of the
Third World and the implications of their predicament for the rest
of the international community have received little attention in
North America and Europe. But this inattention seems extraordinary
when one considers the relation between a variety of Third World
energy possibilities and the issues of foreign policy, development
strategy, and finance with which they are entangled. These relation-
ships are not limited in their importance to those who feel sympathy
for the Third World's energy predicament. They are germane—in this
book we argue they are essential—to efforts in the 1980s to shape
new energy strategies in both Western and developing countries.

The Western industrial countries can help develop new energy sources in the Third World and in so doing, stabilize their own economic systems. The OPEC states can stabilize their political alliances and diversify their investments. It is both ironic and troubling that governments have failed to act decisively upon the threat to their own well-being that is carried forward by the deepening energy crisis of the world's poor countries. To try to explain this failure in full would require another book, covering a much wider range of relations between states. However, at least one contributing factor is the widespread ignorance and misunderstanding of the potential benefits of energy cooperation with the Third World.

This book evaluates the international problems and the potentialities for stimulating new energy initiatives for the benefit of developing countries of the Third World.[a] Energy and poverty are both politically charged subjects. Combined, they offer a formidably explosive potential. So it is as well that we clarify at the outset the political perceptions on which our analysis is based.

Energy issues generate intensely nationalistic concern. This is true among the countries of the Organization for Economic Cooperation and Development (OECD), where no issue has been more divisive than European irritation at America's inability to slow down significantly the rate at which it imports and consumes oil. It is equally true among the "Group of 77," the loose political affiliation of Third World countries, including the Organization of Petroleum Exporting Countries (OPEC), that now numbers 129 states which are held together by large geopolitical issues such as a new economic order for the Third World or the Palestine question, the "Group of 77"'s unity has on more than one occasion been strained almost to the breaking point by the fact that the poorest countries have been hurt most by OPEC price increases.[b] Indeed, the determination of bargaining groups among states (particularly the "North" and "South") to maintain solidarity often obscures the great pressures felt within these groups to break ranks in response to more immediate self-interest. The wealthier developing countries have by now achieved

---

[a]Detailed discussion of present institutional arrangements, which have changed little in recent years, are available elsewhere, as are extensive, if inconclusive, evaluations of technological alternatives to which institutions and governments might now turn. (See Bibliography, p. 197).

[b]The Organization for Economic Cooperation and Development (OECD) is a loose affiliation of twenty-four Western industrialized countries and Japan, headquartered in Paris, that provides a forum for concerted planning and—occasionally—action by its members. The "Group of 77" as such has no formal organization.

a large measure of self-reliance and bargaining power; the poorest have almost none whatever with which to influence the outside world, and in particular the type of concessional help available to them. But the attempt of the vulnerable, oil-poor Third World to mitigate their evident weakness behind a guise of Third World energy solidarity is becoming damaging to their own interests.

This situation parallels another political development of the 1970s, the increasing strain not only among but also *within* so many of the less developed countries (LDCs). The official aid strategy of Western donors and lenders has increasingly focused upon the needs of the poorest people in the poorest countries—the estimated 800 million whose existence is permanently at risk because their fundamental or "basic" human needs remain unmet. To reach these people, donors of aid must work within national economic systems. But these systems often show scant signs of bridging the social chasm between their own rich and poor, and equally little concern with doing so. This is often especially true in the smaller, poorer countries of the Third World—precisely the ones that must inevitably rely most on outside help in planning and delivering sources of energy to the poorest strata of their societies.

Finally attempts to tackle such issues through world conferences and global institutions, simply has the effect of institutionalizing conflicts. In the case of energy, national interests are so compelling that easing international antagonism requires much more than institutionalized responses. It demands a general change in assumptions and expectations.

In the end, of course, options for energy aid to the Third World must be measured within the limits of political reality and available energy resources. We therefore have tried to evaluate present efforts and future prospects for energy investment in developing countries, and its relationship to aid, from several perspectives:

1. What is really at stake for the North, for OPEC, and for the developing countries?
2. What energy alternatives are available for investment now, and what are the outstanding potentials and disadvantages of each?
3. What types of programs are being promoted and funded by aid institutions and government agencies, and how effective are they?
4. In light of the active interest taken by a growing Northern solar energy industry in developing country markets, what is its potential contribution to energy cooperation, and what are the limitations of its involvement?

5. How well equipped are developing countries to take all of these circumstances into account and to coordinate the activities of outsiders in their own best interest?

※ *Chapter 1*

The International Politics of
Energy Cooperation

The political triangle formed by the major oil exporters, the poor South, and the rich, but economically depressed, North has remained in uncreative deadlock since the first great surge of oil price increases of 1973. Each side is hurt by this stalemate. Its origin is well known. It lies in the extent to which life in the industrial North is hooked on oil and the fact that rapid change to less dependence is impossible. Moreover, the will to change has so far been largely wanting. Surveys show that many Americans and a number of Europeans are still refusing to recognize the market implications of excessive oil demand. Either profiteering U.S. and European oil companies or the Organization of Petroleum Exporting Countries—OPEC—are still widely blamed. But if the cause of the stalemate has become clearer, the damage that is being done to the interests of the triangle's two powerful corners—OPEC and the industrial North—by failing to help the weakest corner—the oil-importing South—has not been fully appreciated. The path of confrontation has thus not only failed since 1973 to check oil price rises, but it has also added greatly to existing suspicions, with the result that each side of the triangle formed by the separate interests of North, OPEC, and South has suffered and caused suffering to the others.

THE TRIANGLE OF SUSPICION

Taking the North-OPEC axis first (which, from the standpoint of strategy, resolves itself into the question of North Atlantic-Arab rela-

5

tions), the 1980s open with ominous new risks of escalation arising from diplomatic and military pressure. Recent events in Iran and Afghanistan increase the likelihood that, with the Vietnam entanglement now distant in the public memory, American leadership will be tempted to confrontation and the threat of military action to secure oil supplies from the Middle East at "affordable" cost. Such a strategy cannot be discounted in the coming decade, or for as long as oil remains a strategically vital resource, particularly if the United States were to reach some private accommodation with the Soviet Union, whose direct interest in the region is bound to grow, not only because of Arab irridentism but because of East European need for Arab oil.

Soviet interests in access to warm water ports and its forecast demand for Middle Eastern oil by the mid-1980s could well combine with growing Russian nervousness over the implications of Islamic militancy among the 50 million Soviet Muslims who largely populate the southern republics of the Soviet Union and whose populations are growing at a much faster rate than those of the USSR's "European" republics. In this respect, Soviet concern about events in Iran and its intervention in Afghanistan, though quite different in origin, parallel U.S. fears over secure oil supplies. Either a Soviet reach to the south or a superpower deal over spheres of influence cannot be ruled out; indeed, if the lessons of history are to be learned, these emerge as distinct, and perhaps not even distant, possibilities. Such a prospect cannot be discounted when one considers that supposedly "unthinkable" events have become the norm in the oil-rich "horn of crisis."

On the axis of the industrial North and oil-poor South, the impact of the energy crisis has been almost equally corrosive of trust. Every major encounter of the "North-South dialogue" during the last half of the 1970s has disappointed all of the concerned parties, and in many cases these sessions have appeared to founder over energy issues. The North-South dialogue has become shorthand for a series of governmental and international meetings convened during the period since 1974, when the United Nations General Assembly adopted a "Declaration on the Establishment of a New International Economic Order (NIEO)." The NIEO calls for the restructuring of the international monetary system as well as of the terms on which raw materials and commodities are bought and sold and the means of transferring technology from North to South. This Southern initiative might never have reached the negotiating table (it still has not been seriously negotiated) were it not that the rich industrial North

was searching desperately for a forum for negotiating a new international *energy* order. The OPEC Summit Conference of March 1975
bound the two agendas together. It thus ensured—or was supposed to
ensure—that the North would listen to other Third World proposals.

The consequent Conference on International Economic Cooperation (CIEC)—the focal point of the North-South dialogue—met in
Paris from December 1975 through June 1977 and divided its work
into four commissions, one of which concerned energy. Whether the
tense energy discussions crippled the entire CIEC is debatable. What
is clear, however, is that no significant agreements on energy matters
were reached. Discussions about prices, financial assistance to oil-
importing developing countries, and recycling of "petrodollars" left
rancor in their wake.

Furthermore, efforts to give energy cooperation the continuity of
an institutional structure, perhaps by creating an International
Energy Institute, failed completely in the CIEC, as did later efforts
within the U.N. system to promote the IEI proposal. Finally, and
most recently, Mexico's attempts to review international energy
discussions outside the context of general economic talks met with
polite disfavor from the developing countries, which, in the view
of Mexican President López Portillo, might have expected to benefit
most from the talks. Again, the oil-importing Third World refused to
separate energy questions from the overall terms of trade, debt, and
technology transfer "package" of the NIEO.

The suspicion reflected in these negative attitudes on the part of
the oil-poor developing countries is readily understandable when one
considers the immense inequities in the present structure of international trade and technology transfer. One must also take into account that poor countries are naturally wary of a possible political
split with OPEC, should OPEC take the view that they were prepared
to make separate energy deals with the West.

In spite of evident strains on Third World unity caused by oil price
increases, in international forums the developing countries as a whole
generally support OPEC positions for the sake of preserving Third
World solidarity. Their reasoning results from OPEC's movement to
the center of the world stage in the years since 1973. In that year,
OPEC nations were hailed by other Third World countries as cham-
pions who had redefined the terms of North-South economic relations. But since then, other Third World nations have discovered that
non-oil commodities have little, if any, of the leverage provided by
oil. The oil exporters' success has not been duplicated, and it has encountered growing disfavor ever since, for example, at the Novem-

ber 1979 meeting of oil-importing Third World countries held in Kingston, Jamaica, under the auspices of the United Nations Conference on Trade and Development (UNCTAD). Poorer countries have been increasingly eager to discuss oil prices and have only held back in exchange for the promise of consultations in the near future.

This is not to say that the Third World's oil exporters have left all pleas unheeded. There are signs, for example, of an increasing focus of Arab development aid programs on energy projects. OPEC members agreed in June 1979 to an $800-million replenishment of the OPEC Fund, to be used for "energy aid," and at the December 1979 OPEC conference in Caracas, they agreed in principle to double that amount. 1. Many Western commentators maintain that OPEC's generosity has never approached a scale commensurate with the hardship created by OPEC oil prices. However, it must in fairness be recalled that oil cartelization was a fact under the dominance of the oil majors (the "seven sisters") long before OPEC. Moreover, the OPEC members now provide over a quarter of official development aid, and 10–15 per cent of other capital flows to the oil importing Third World. OPEC aid in 1979 was almost seven times higher, as a percentage of national income than that of the United States. Despite the fact that OPEC's recent new aid commitments (in 1980) represent less than the amount by which it increased the LDCs' oil bill at a stroke most oil-poor developing countries remain unwilling to contemplate a breach with the oil exporters for historical and geopolitical reasons. They continue to believe that only their political solidarity with OPEC lends force to their more general demands for international economic reform.

However, on the oil-poor Third World–OPEC side of the triangle there is mounting tension born of desperation. Only when all three corners of the triangle understand the cost to each of refusing to recognize these separate group interests concerning energy supply will the price of suspicion in terms of a downward world economic spiral and mounting threats of political breakdown and military confrontation be fully counted and rejected.

THE PRICE OF SUSPICION

There is still little recognition among the general public of the West of how closely the economic fortunes, and especially the energy prospects, of the industrial and the oil-importing poor nations are tied together.

Costs to the North

As it examines the implications of Third World energy problems, the most immediate political concern for the industrialized North must be over the impact of the Third World's inability to pay its growing oil debts on the international financial system and a slumping world economy. In four years (1973 to early 1978) the foreign debt of the Third World, excluding OPEC, increased from an estimated $93 billion to $210 billion. These nations owe $190 billion to private institutions, and this amount does not reflect the impact of 1979 oil price increases. Much, though by no means all, of this debt derives from loans for the purchase of oil (or for the planned increase of cash reserves, hedging against further oil price rises), that the private banking community is now extremely concerned at the delicacy of their position. Indeed, early in 1980, with inadequate equity capital to back the risk element in recycling Arab surpluses, some major American banks were refusing further deposits. The scale of debt has reached such proportions that it has been said to grow automatically as countries borrow to finance the servicing of their existing loans. Current intellectual paralysis in the face of this growing oil debt was apparent on all sides in Manila at the fifth session of the United Nations Conference on Trade and Development. As the *Economist* observed, "What is one to say of an international gathering which, in May 1979, could contemplate a lengthy resolution on the world economy that deliberately excluded the word 'energy'?"[1]

Interdependence of economic health between the West and the Third World makes the Third World's oil indebtedness all the more critical. The United States, for example, now earns more from its exports to developing countries, including OPEC nations, than it does from those of the Common Market, Japan, and the Communist countries combined. Oil-pinched buying power in developing countries can eliminate jobs in the West and hits particularly hard in certain areas. Four of the state of Washington's biggest customers are developing countries, and such economic ties are even closer for several members of the European Community, particularly France and Britain.

The Politics of Nuclear Delay

The issue of jobs and export customers is particularly intractable in the area of exported nuclear power. The United States and its Western allies have disagreed as to whether slowing down the spread of nuclear reactors in the Third World will in turn limit the spread of nuclear weapons. But it is now clear that any effective non-proliferation policy must be accompanied by help in planning national energy programs: Indeed, even the most extreme European opponents of President Carter's non-proliferation policy can hardly argue that Third World countries should not be helped to make economically sound energy choices.

Unhappily, however, the nuclear non-proliferation policy was better conceived than it was presented. Its strategy was to prevent a premature commitment to nuclear power (particularly to advanced fuel-cycle systems that produce weapons-grade nuclear materials) in the hope that improved international safeguards could be agreed upon, or that new technology would permit "proliferation-resistant" nuclear reactors. In the developing countries in particular, another hope for any nuclear non-proliferation strategy remains the likelihood that with each passing year the *economic* case in favor of alternatives to nuclear power will grow stronger, sufficiently strong, indeed, to discourage any Third World leaders, except those with the strongest political and strategic motives, from wanting nuclear weapons—a small minority who must inevitably be dealt with (if they can be dissuaded at all) by other sorts of bilateral political argument.

This strategy of "nuclear delay" can only work, however, if developing countries focus on an economically realistic range of energy choices. The U.S. government has initiated programs to accomplish that objective, but it is not surprising that the announced motive for these efforts (non-proliferation) initially threatened their acceptability, and hence their effectiveness.

Energy and the Geopolitics of Environmental Destruction

The most politically remote but perhaps, in the long run, compelling motive for rethinking energy aid to developing countries arises out of the convergence of environmental problems associated with global development. Though far from public attention, the interconnecting problems of deforestation, soil loss, agricultural depletion, and climatic change will, if uncontrolled, produce crisis conditions and global disruptions not many years hence, which, by that time, would scarcely be susceptible to technological ingenuity for their solution, on whatever scale it was applied. This emerging dilemma is not limited in its effects to Third World countries facing these specific problems. Protracted food shortages, for example, would certainly threaten the stability on which so much of Western investment relies. Global deforestation is progressing so rapidly that it may affect the balance of carbon dioxide in the atmosphere.

In an age of growing sophistication and instant global communication, it is perhaps possible that the people of industrialized countries and their leadership will see the vital connection between these problems and the impact of scarce energy on the global environment. For even though the day of reckoning on many world resource problems connected with energy may seem safely distant, in the West the public is becoming aware of the fragile interconnectedness of natural systems and aware that survival, not only for poor countries but for their own future generations as well, may be at stake. But whether the immediate environmental threat to developing countries, and its longer term implications for developed countries, can be linked forcefully enough in the public's mind to support major foreign policy efforts in these areas remains an unhappily doubtful question.

Costs to the Oil-Poor South

If the energy crisis of the Third World affects the prospects of the dominant industrial North, the effect in the oil-poor countries concerned is infinitely more devastating.

The escalating oil prices of the 1970s put oil-importing Third World countries into a peculiarly painful double bind. In these countries, the actual cost of commercial fuel, especially in rural areas, almost invariably exceeds prices paid in the industrialized nations (due to high transportation costs, particularly for those that are landlocked). But a different kind of price—the rapid destruction of natural resources—is paid by the majority of people in most of the Third World who still rely entirely for their energy supply on rapidly disappearing traditional fuels like firewood and charcoal.[a] Thus almost every developing country faces some variation of the North's energy crisis and at the same time confronts a problem unique to the poorest segments of its society. The combination of these two elements has at least four distinct effects.

First, the financial impact. As we have seen, the international financial position of oil-importing developing countries as a whole is precarious. An increasing share of their national wealth is devoted to paying oil bills, and growth, as a result, has slowed dramatically in a number of countries (down from an average of 7.6 percent to 3.0 percent between 1973 and 1975). At the same time, the credit of most of the poor developing countries is stretched far beyond the limits of realistic capacity to repay. A string of African and Asian nations now verge on bankruptcy. Tanzania, for example, has recently announced emergency measures to cut its national oil consumption by *50 percent*. Brazil's entire economy has been under-

---

[a]For a vivid indication of the extent to which populations of the poorest countries rely on traditional or "noncommercial" fuels, see Figure 1, p. 12.

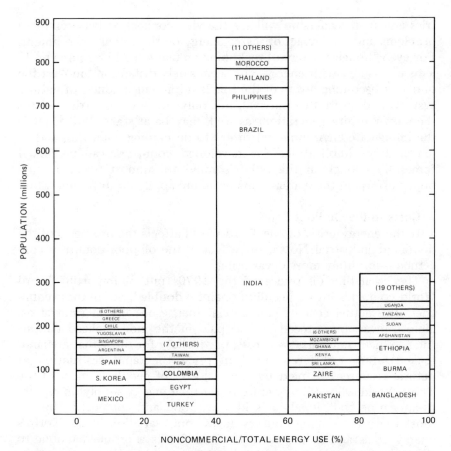

Figure 1. Noncommercial Energy Use[a] as a Percentage of Total Energy Use, versus Population, by Country

SOURCES:
1974 (est.) Population (Table 18, *U.N. Statistical Yearbook 1975.*)
Commercial Energy Use: (*U.N. World Energy Supplies 1971–1975*, 1977)
Noncommercial Energy Use: 400 kgce/ rural population

NOTE: Reproduced from Philip F. Palmedo, Robert Nathans, Edward Beardsworth, Samuel Hale Jr., et al., *Energy Needs, Uses and Resources in Developing Countries* (Upton, N.Y.: Brookhaven National Laboratory, 1978) p. 68, Figure C–1. Reprinted with permission.

[a]*Noncommercial*, or *traditional*, energy sources are defined in this figure as those widely used in preindustrial economies, that is, energy sources that are not normally bought and sold. The noncommercial or traditional category generally includes woodfuels, crop residues, animal dung, animal draft power, and direct solar energy for drying. Human muscle power, wind, and small-scale hydro may also be included in the calculations.

mined by its oil debts. These countries now find it very difficult to obtain international credit on top of their existing debts, especially from the International Monetary Fund (IMF), which attaches strict conditions to its credits.

An indication of the financial burden imposed by oil purchases is given by measuring the cost of energy imports (oil, gas, coal, etc.) as a percentage of merchandise export earnings. For low-income developing countries, energy imports jumped from 9 percent of merchandise export earnings in 1960 to 19 percent in 1975. For middle-income countries, the percentage grew from 10 percent in 1960 to 22 percent in 1975. The industrialized-country figures for the same period are about the same (in 1975, 24 percent of merchandise export earnings went to pay for energy imports), but they have had a comparatively smaller impact. This is because merchandise earnings constitute a much greater part of total Third World export earnings than is the case with industrialized countries, where export of services provides substantial income.[2] The implications of inhibited Third World buying power at a time of world recession are not the most direct link between the energy crises of North and South, but, as the report of the Brandt Commission points out, they are perhaps the most significant one.[3]

Second, the impact of rising fuel bills on productivity is greater in developing countries than in the United States or Europe, because economic growth in the modern sense (statistically measured by gross national product) is firmly locked onto a path that increases or decreases with oil consumption. For example, the prospect of obtaining electric power from a grid is being denied to more and more people. The increasing cost of generating and transmitting electric power removes its benefits further not only from the poorest members of society but from small urban centers and farmers in rural areas whose productivity could be immensely increased by access to it.

Third, the social impact of the increasing scarcity of firewood directly threatens both the quality of life and life itself. In the countryside, in many developing countries, the waking hours of women, and especially children, are occupied by the ever more time-consuming task of gathering wood. In some cities to which firewood

---

Today most of these sources are bought and sold in developing countries, and in the future this will be increasingly so. Therefore the commercial/non-commercial nomenclature is not entirely accurate, although most authors continue to use it for lack of more precise terminology.

In practice, noncommercial fuels include all but fossil fuels and electricity produced from conversion of fossil fuels, nuclear fission, or hydropower.

and charcoal are now shipped from great distances, their purchase consumes as much as 30 to 40 percent of poor people's annual incomes.

Fourth, a massive increase in damage—often long-term or permanent—to renewable resources (especially to food supplies) arises from the fuelwood crisis. One of the heaviest impacts of higher oil prices has been the removal of kerosene for cooking from the reach of those people (particularly in urban areas) whose need for additional firewood augments the pressure on brush and woodlands. The consequent loss of soil through desertification and erosion threatens food supplies in many areas, and in some countries, such as India, the burning of animal dung as a wood substitute has seriously depleted the supply of natural fertilizer.[b]

All of these conditions are exacerbated because the developing countries as a whole are even more dependent on oil than the larger Western consumers. Forty-eight of the seventy-four developing countries that import oil depend upon liquid fuels for at least 90 percent of their commercial energy (twenty-nine of these are in Africa, twelve in the Western Hemisphere, two in the Middle East, and five in Asia).[4] This compares to a 77 percent reliance on liquid fuels for the nations of the Organization for Economic Cooperation and De-

---

[b]It is often added that the threat to food supplies has been compounded by the price of the oil-based feedstock of artificial fertilizer. However, it must be remembered that almost all of the poorest live outside the "fertilizer economy." Moreover, this argument has frequently been overemphasized and has drawn attention away from the far more serious problem of soil loss. The very sharp (4–5 times) increase in fertilizer prices in 1973–74 was primarily caused by world food shortages in 1973 and the subsequent explosion in demand for nitrogen fertilizers. In 1975, however, as supply rose to meet demand, artificial fertilizer costs fell in real terms and have been low relative to oil price increases since. In large part, this has been due to the massive increase in fertilizer production from low-cost natural gas in the Middle East and elsewhere in the developing world.

In addition, the potential energy demand of modernizing Third World agriculture is not nearly as great as is often suggested. It has been calculated, for example, that if all developing countries were to treble their use of nitrogen fertilizers, this would only imply an additional 56 million tons of oil equivalent per year, which represents 10 percent of all developing-country energy use, or 1 percent of world fuel supply. By the same token, if *all* draft animals in Third World agriculture were to be replaced by oil-fueled tractors, they would consume only 10 million tons of oil per year. (This argument is explained in detail in the draft report of "Agricultural Production: Research and Development Strategies for the 1980s," August 1979, prepared by the Energy Resources Working Group of the Bonn International Conference.) The essential point remains, however, that such alternatives are not, today, open to the landless peasant without access to credit, and he is therefore still likely to rob the soil of natural nutrition by burning animal dung as a wood substitute, or to produce soil erosion by taking firewood.

velopment (OECD) as a whole.[5] As a result, even though commercial energy represents a relatively small proportion of total energy consumed when compared to developed countries, these countries are hurt more than any others by oil price increases.

In light of these and similar circumstances in so many less developed countries, one might have expected some sort of alliance, even one sub rosa, among oil importers of North and South alike. That this has not happened has, as the Brandt Commission pointed out, not only damaged the interests of the South but also greatly increased economic dangers faced by the North.

Costs to the Oil Exporters

What price, then, do the oil-exporting countries pay for being party to the triangle of suspicion? The threat to their economies grows with the world recession. The risk of armed conflict, especially in the Middle East, has been touched upon already. Less obvious, but in the long run as dangerous, is the damage to their interests from growing hardship, tension, and economic and environmental disruption in the poorer parts of the oil-importing Third World. Together these factors, when coupled with the American obsession over oil price and quotas, have exacerbated the present sterile deadlock.

Could OPEC not have responded to the Third World's dogged, if increasingly wistful, solidarity with a structure of concessional oil pricing for badly hit developing countries? Perhaps, but the question unfairly shifts too much of the burden to OPEC. Should they be expected to behave with a level of altruism on a different order of magnitude from that of historically well-off developed countries? Moreover, poor countries' appeal for OPEC funds have to be realistically considered in light of these countries' capacity to absorb and use the resources fruitfully to further their economic development.

What are the oil-exporting states' reasons for standing pat? The first thing to be remembered when speaking of the oil-exporting group is their extreme disparity of character. Any coalition that binds together Venezuela, Libya, and Saudi Arabia cannot be expected to share all foreign policy goals, or indeed many other goals of national policy. Nevertheless, oil can be a powerful political adhesive. The underlying strategy of many OPEC states, especially the major "moderate" Arab producers, is to leave as much oil as possible in the ground for the time being. The Arabs have few other valuable resources and genuinely want to leave an income for future generations. OPEC economies have also been able to absorb or recycle their increased national revenues much more smoothly than was expected five years ago, largely through vastly expanded import programs.

They are therefore not searching the non-oil Third World for investment opportunities. Their interest in this type of foreign investment is limited, too, by their unease at the traps and pitfalls that beset the rich foreign investor in a poor country environment, particularly the inexperienced rich foreign investor. Besides, OPEC countries have set as their first priority the building of viable industrial economies at home, and this effort, together with investments in North America and Western Europe and with massive arms and aircraft purchases, has absorbed the bulk of their new oil wealth.

The most obvious OPEC concession would involve a system of two-tiered oil prices, with the lower tier set according to poor countries' ability to pay. This approach is, however, mistrusted by OPEC since it would be bound to create a massive black market arising from international resale of the oil. After all, funds with which to finance imports or repay debts are even more urgently needed by the poorest countries than more oil. Under a worldwide two-tier system, not only would the cheap oil be diverted away from its intended beneficiaries, but OPEC would lose a measure of control over its distribution. The major oil companies would regain much of their recently reduced influence. Another reason for OPEC hesitation at setting up concessional oil pricing reflects OPEC's vehement repudiation of the principle that OPEC aid represents compensation for an economic injury. In fact, some individual OPEC members, such as Kuwait, little of whose oil supplies developing countries, have long given far more in development assistance than non-oil Third World countries have lost through OPEC pricing policies. As a result, there is little interest among OPEC members in general to any direct linking of their aid to any notion of compensation for an economic injury. This reluctance is also encouraged by the fact that the control of the destiny of about 60 per cent of their oil exports is still in the hands of international oil companies, even though this control is rapidly shifting hands.[c]

The events of 1979, the worsening of world inflation and recession, as well as more immediate pressure on OPEC at UNCTAD V in Havana, in the United Nations, and elsewhere—all these factors indicate that if the oil exporters want to preserve their Third World

---

[c]Venezuela, which sells a significant proportion of its oil to developing countries, is an exception. The Venezuelan Investment Fund was set up in 1974 to promote a variety of development financing schemes. One program commits Venezuela to deposit a fixed proportion of oil revenue from Latin American importers into the central bank of the importing country, for redistribution as development assistance loans.

alliances they must do more. They need to honor their commitment to meet the immediate problems of those hardest hit, as well as to help poor countries plan for the post-oil era. Herein lies the potential convergence of interest with the Western industrial democracies.

AN OPPORTUNITY FOR CONVERGENCE

Just because they *are* still undeveloped industrially, the development patterns and strategies that appear to lock many Third World countries into their present pattern of energy use are not, in fact, as entrenched as they might appear. In industrialized countries, the established commitment of vast amounts of capital to a particular production and consumption infrastructure (in short, the commitment of the entire community to a particular lifestyle) dramatically narrows the choices that politicians are willing to consider. But developing country leaders are contending not so much with habit as with aspiration. *How* the hopes for a better life are met may be less important than the belief that they will be fulfilled. Very little has yet been done, however, to establish and clarify choices for developing countries among alternative energy sources and technologies.

These countries face a dilemma: Should they try to adapt to the new energy realities by organizing new national energy plans and encouraging the design of energy supply systems in accord with an admittedly imperfect knowledge of alternative technological potentials, but at least based upon their own perceptions of their needs? Or should they wait until the price of oil coupled with other outside pressures (for example from energy technology salesmen or Western consultants) forces decisions upon them, perhaps less appropriate to their own perceptions of their needs? How they will respond to this dilemma is of course uncertain. What seems increasingly likely however, is that Third World leaders will accept, at first hesitantly, new energy priorities. Some of these are now emerging in Western aid agencies—and in Western governments generally—as they try to shift away from oil.

New Thinking on Energy Aid

The trend of the 1970s to target economic aid on the poorest sectors of developing societies implies—and indeed requires—a new perception of energy's role in development. There are many signs that a change along these lines is getting under way. But energy planners and development strategists still have far to go, particularly in devising programs that reach those whose energy demands are undermining the natural resource base of their national economies. Until quite recently, energy aid has been almost exclusively devoted to the generation and transmission of electric power.

The conventional path of oil-fired electric power generation and rural electrification was understood by planners, and indeed seen by Third World populations generally, as the route that must inevitably be followed to achieve the widespread benefits of a modern industrialized economy. The equation of Third World development with urban-based industrial expansion dictated this emphasis and guided the concentration of international finance in the energy field to large electricity supply projects, which have increasingly included an element of rural electrification. So total has been this commitment that in 1979 the total sum being spent by *all* nations on solar energy research (to take just one example from several promising alternative energy sources) was still less than the cost of building a single 1,000-megawatt nuclear power station.

Thus energy aid in the late 1970s—in part because of long-term commitments to major electric power schemes—largely failed to register the new general commitment to the poorest. However, the impetus behind a realignment of energy strategies is growing rapidly now in most developed countries, and particularly in the United States. Donors of aid are beginning to argue that the concept of a New International Economic Order cannot be applied internationally unless it is applied domestically as well, and, as is indicated in Chapter 3, this logic is also beginning to be applied to energy programs. This is not to foresee or expect that there will be, or that there ought to be, a sudden and dramatic switch of development resources from energy for the modern sector to decentralized energy for the rural poor. Such a *volte face* is neither politically possible not economically feasible. Moreover, from the viewpoint of the self-interest of the industrial North, further investment in conventional energy sources— oil, gas, coal, hydropower (nuclear power being bracketed by both safety and economic question marks)—helps to reduce pressure on present known reserves of nonrenewable resources for rich as well as poor countries. As such it should be welcomed by all. Foreign investment in such conventional projects, with its obvious benefits to today's major oil consumers, should not, however, be counted as "aid." This term is more properly applied to those energy investments that reach and alleviate the lot of the very poor, and help them to avoid destroying the natural resource and environmental infrastructure on which their countries must rely now and in the decades ahead.

At present, the overall energy planning and management institutions of oil-poor developing countries are either weak or nonexistent (as is often the case in the West and the oil-exporting Third World as well). Unless they can develop the capacity for such planning and management, the transfer of new technologies, especially for renewable energy supplies, is going to be seriously impeded.

No Third World country is going to accept unquestioningly a new energy strategy dictated from outside. Aid programs must, then, devote increased resources to help with training and "institution building," so that poor countries can map their own path in a new global energy order. If national energy planning and technical capabilities can be strengthened, then there is every chance that many developing countries will manage to bypass the trap of complete fossil fuel dependence. Without such independent decisionmaking and strategic skills, however, innovations that may emerge from Northern industry and aid programs will make little significant headway in the developing world.

COSTS AND BENEFITS
OF NEW INITIATIVES

During 1979, the U.S. Secretary of State and the President of the World Bank each devoted a major speech to emphasizing the urgency of helping the "non-oil" Third World to devise solutions to its unique energy predicament. But as might have been expected, they approached the issues differently. Bank President McNamara emphasized humanitarian as well as economic grounds, whereas Secretary Vance (speaking to a U.S. trade group) tried to demonstrate the immediate economic interdependence of his audience with its developing country markets. Later, speaking to the United Nations General Assembly, Vance reiterated that "we recognize that by helping others resolve their energy problems, we help resolve our own."

Getting public assent to helping developing countries with energy is difficult and challenging, both because of considerable apathy over aid generally and because there remains the dispiriting recognition—in North and South alike—that nations that seem to be making so little progress toward solving their own energy problems are perhaps not ideally qualified to offer advice to others. Nevertheless, an appealing argument with Western politicians is that helping the Third World to meet its energy needs will release more oil for aid-giving countries. In this view there is both truth and the dangerous possibility of a backlash if developing countries interpret it to mean "you use solar power, but it is too unsophisticated for us," or even (as could happen in the coming years) "you bear the cost and risks of

nuclear power while we use the oil." Likewise, any assumption that
poor populations only need enough energy to sustain frugal lifestyles
could also undermine new energy cooperation efforts. Probably the
best way to avoid suspicious, or indeed hostile, Third World reactions
to "alternative" energy aid is to promote programs whose clear intention is first and foremost to help the Third World.

Take the example of oil. Few parts of the Third World have over
past decades escaped the attentions of commercial oil prospectors.
But much of this surveying was done on two related assumptions.
The first was that the reserves had to be of a size suitable for exploitation for the international market—and therefore large. The
second was that oil prices would remain in their traditional relationship to other costs. Neither assumption remains valid today.
Moreover, today's exploration and recovery technology renders
the work of earlier prospectors largely redundant. Thus there is
now increasing interest in relatively small scale oil exploration and
production in non-OPEC developing countries (such as recently has
been inaugurated by the World Bank). Such developments could
moderate Third World dependency on oil imports very significantly.
Programs of such development are only likely to be acceptable, however, if institutional arrangements for their implementation, while
gaining initial advice and technical assistance from oil companies,
and indeed from the OPEC states, remain firmly in the hands of the
nations concerned.

This accepted, we should note that there remains substantial disagreement about the potential effect, in the industrialized countries,
of increased Third World non-OPEC oil production. A recent U.S.
report summarized the contending views: "Although some experts
feel that the undiscovered oil fields will be small, they do not all
agree that all future finds will be too small for export potential".[6]
Thus it is important that developing countries, Western aid donors,
and suppliers of oil technology realize that new oil and gas programs
may not do a great deal to reduce upward pressure on world oil
prices, at least for the foreseeable future. This could only be achieved,
if at all, if the West were to moderate its demand for oil through conservation and substitution. The real advantage for developed countries of oil assistance programs such as that inaugurated by the World
Bank, in addition to the reduction of the Third World's disastrous
balance of payments deficit, is in diversifying the supply of oil in
international markets regardless of price. This becomes particularly
important in the decade ahead, in the light of Saudi Arabia's announced decision never to increase production beyond 12 million
barrels per day, regardless of technical capacity or demand.

Obviously, the West is likely to derive other benefits from efforts to improve energy-use efficiency and to hasten the transition to new sources of energy in developing countries. Manufacturers of solar equipment, for example, believe that a substantial market exists for their products in the Third World (see Chapter 4). Although the "terms of transfer" of technology have become a highly sensitive issue between North and South, it should be possible to provide renewable energy aid to developing countries on mutually agreeable terms. However, it is important to recognize that renewable (particularly solar energy) technologies that attract Western investment will not necessarily correspond to the focus of *aid* programs. Solar air conditioning for luxury hotels, might, for example, prove to be a profitable, cooperative energy innovation that could help some countries to earn much-needed foreign exchange. It should, perhaps, receive the initial stimulus of concessional finance, but it should not compete for priority with aid money earmarked for the very poor.

LARGE OPPORTUNITY, LOW POLITICAL COST?

Can Western nations muster the will and the imagination to cooperate among themselves and with OPEC to deal with a dismal list of interlocking problems? OPEC states have no reason to oppose the gradual redirection of Western energy resources in the Third World. In fact it seems clear from our enquiries that if Western nations start doing more they will find a willingness for further cooperation among OPEC states. Moreover, the non-renewable oil resources of most OPEC states are being depleted so rapidly that, as one Third World analyst noted, "in two decades or so they [OPEC] are not likely to have alternative technologies when their energy needs will have increased considerably and there is not likely to be much oil left for export and domestic use."[7] Recent commitments show that some OPEC states are, however, ready to invest in renewable energy resources, particularly to gain access to advanced technologies (which may not be directly applicable to developing country needs, but which are adaptable for many purposes).

We have also stressed that most OPEC members are determined to keep as much oil as possible in the ground for future generations. Kuwait, for example, may systematically reduce its production over the next five years until output has been reduced by half, so as to extend the life of reserves. (This also postpones inflation-driven erosion of Kuwait's international purchasing power.) In these circumstances, it makes great sense for oil-exporting nations to acquire access to, and expertise in, the new energy technologies for their own purposes. For their part, Western purveyors of renewable energy technology have nothing to fear in accepting the oil exporters as financial partners in new energy ventures.

Concern over economic "future shock" is another factor that must encourage the moderates among OPEC's membership, particularly Saudi Arabia, to help finance a wide range of alternative energy sources. If the transition away from oil dependence is postponed, and is therefore less gradual when it occurs, the economic shock of efforts to substitute other energy sources will damage OPEC nations as much as everyone else, especially through depreciation of their Western investments. This could easily happen in economic terms, but there are also grounds for fearing a worldwide oil panic on political, and perhaps military, grounds. Thus it is manifestly in their own interest to palliate the secondary shocks of their oil policies to the extent that the OPEC nations themselves are threatened.

When we presented these considerations to officials from oil-exporting countries, their response suggested that a number of them may react favorably to initiatives opening up greater investment and cooperative opportunities in renewable energy technologies, particularly if the poor countries hurt by oil price rises were identified as the primary beneficiaries. They would do so because they recognize that improving economic conditions in the Third World—the longer run aim of this process—would benefit the oil-rich Third World and the West because it would complement efforts to reduce the political and security tensions that now pervade world energy use.

COMPONENTS OF A STRATEGY

The greatest problem with new energy aid programs is that they have not been conceived in relation to new perceptions in overall development strategy, nor in relation to the long-term crisis in global energy supplies. The Brandt Commission, reporting in February 1980,[8] offered the outlines of a global energy strategy, which it put forward as "a matter of the utmost urgency." The main lines of the strategy are "an accommodation between oil-producing and -consuming countries which can ensure more secure supplies, more rigorous conservation, more predictable changes of prices, and more positive measures to develop alternative sources of energy." The strategy calls upon major energy-consuming countries to commit themselves to agreed and quite specific targets of reduced consumption of oil and other energy, which should be more ambitious than they agreed to at the Tokyo summit meeting in 1979, and these should be accepted and monitored: an agreement to eschew sudden major increases in oil prices, with the longer term target of price indexation or relation to world inflation; major investment in oil and natural gas exploration and development in the Third World countries; and planning and funds for a range of other energy research and development activities. Special new facilities or capacities must be created, the Brandt Commission suggested, to handle the menacing and still growing level of Third World debt. These recommendations are unexceptionable, but they are disappointingly vague and general in the context of the top priority given to them by the Brandt Commission.

Of course, in a chaotic and fast-changing world, it is foolhardy to attempt more than to suggest a common approach. In the chapters that follow, we discuss existing technologies, organizations, and programs that must be employed in the implementation of a strategy for energy cooperation with the Third World. Not all programs will work, of course; not all apparently good ideas will take root. But, more than anything else, the suspicious triangle needs a clearer strategic concept on which to focus common effort.

What are the essential elements of a strategy for energy aid and cooperation?

First, a balanced strategy for energy must involve the search not only for more oil and gas but also for the means of ending the present era of dangerous dependence on fossil energy.

Second, new programs must be based on cooperation, rather than confrontation, with oil-exporting states. Agreements on technology transfer, jointly funded aid projects, and new financing mechanisms are steps in this direction.

Third, the priorities of the non-oil developing countries themselves must influence not only the specific content but also the overall direction of new programs. This points to the very urgent need to train Third World energy researchers and planners, to support indigenous Third World research, and to strengthen developing country institutions charged with energy responsibilities. These are critical first steps without which the best-intentioned strategy will bog down. The developing countries must solve their own energy problems, but the West, in alliance with various of the Arab and other OPEC development funds, can help provide many of the needed tools.

Fourth, new energy programs and policies need to be sensitive to the depletion of critical resources of all varieties, and fragile natural systems that the human race has the power to disrupt permanently. Firewood is running out faster than oil. Many substitute fuels (for firewood *and* for oil) create almost as many problems as they solve.

Any new international energy strategy should therefore stress concern with the protection and regeneration of natural resources.

NOTES

1. *The Economist*, June 9, 1979, p. 85. Reprinted with permission.
2. Source of figures: World Bank, *World Development Report, 1979* (Washington, D.C.: World Bank, 1979).
3. The Independent Commission on International Development Issues (popularly referred to as the Brandt Commission), *North—South: A Programme for Survival* (Cambridge, Massachusetts: The MIT Press, 1980).
4. See Philip F. Palmedo et al., *Energy Needs, Uses and Resources in Developing Countries* (Upton, N.Y.: Brookhaven National Laboratory, 1978), pp. 21–25; also see World Bank, *A Program to Accelerate Petroleum Production in the Developing Countries* (Washington, D.C.: World Bank, January 1979), p. 23.
5. International Energy Agency, *Energy Balances of OECD Countries* (Paris: International Energy Agency-Organization for Economic Cooperation and Development, 1978), p. 56.
6. U.S. General Accounting Office, *Issues Related to Foreign Oil Supply Diversification* (ID-79-36, Washington, D.C.: GAO, May 31, 1979), Appendix I p. 4.
7. See International Consultative Group on Nuclear Energy, *Nuclear Energy and International Cooperation: A Third World View of the Erosion of Confidence* (New York: The Rockefeller Foundation, 1979), p. 17.
8. *North—South: A Programme for Survival.*

※ *Chapter 2*

Energy Sources and Technologies:
Hard Choices

THE TARGETRY PROBLEM

One of the biggest problems facing both Northern aid programs and developing country governments as they set up new energy programs is to get the fullest use out of existing resources that are both limited and constrained. This might be called the problem of "targetry." By this we refer to the series of choices (or biases) among alternative investment opportunities, aid subsidies, and technological options that are made (or implied) before any allocation of resources can be decided upon.

The complexity of these decisions is perhaps illustrated by the case of energy aid to Mali. In fact, a whole range of difficult energy aid choices is illustrated by the concentration of considerable donor country interest in this large, but sparsely populated, desert and semiarid Saharan country. The European Development Fund (EDF— the fast-growing concessional aid program of the European Community) and the U.S. Agency for International Development (AID) have established quite opposite strategies to help ease Mali's acute firewood and oil crisis. Each agency is carrying out a renewable energy project in Mali. The EDF has set up a considerable number of solar energy demonstration projects using irrigation pumps powered by photovoltaic cells.[a] The EDF's representatives in Mali want a

---

[a]Direct photovoltaic conversion of sunlight (the solar spectrum) to electricity can be achieved with basically simple devices that involve no moving parts, no additional sources of energy, and little if any maintenance. These "solar cells" consist of a wafer of crystalline material to which two metal contacts are

highly visible program using the most reliable solar water pumping equipment available. They are installing relatively expensive pumps designed for use by an entire village (the average cost is about $50,000 per pump). The philosophy is that these very low-maintenance, trouble-free units can have a considerable impact on crop irrigation and water supply in the villages. Certainly this approach has attracted publicity and interested the Malian government.

The American energy project in Mali takes an entirely different approach, proceeding in four research and application phases over a period of several years. It includes an overall evaluation of socio-economic factors and villager preferences, as well as research on biogas and solar-powered irrigation.[b] The project is primarily designed to gather and analyze information, rather than to have an immediate effect on the needs of villagers. The eventual goal is described as providing technical and data foundation for future work of AID and the government, so that larger scale projects can be properly planned and executed.

Not surprisingly, each aid agency has considerable reservations about the other's approach. They appear, superficially, to be not only incompatible but mutually frustrating, even to the point that the demonstration effect of the EDF program could render redundant the longer term study of options by AID. But it is possible that *both* approaches are appropriate in the same country at the same time. To attack the energy problems of a country like Mali on the needed scale, political and popular support needs to be generated at every level. Hopes for a better future—the belief that problems are solvable—must be fired. This means early and tangible results. The EDF effort serves these purposes. The AID project will excite nobody other than a few energy and development planners, but it may

---

fastened, which, when the material is exposed to sunlight, produce an electric current.

By contrast, solar thermal devices harness the *heat* from the sun's rays to complete such tasks as heating water, drying crops, desalinizing water, heating and cooling buildings, or producing mechanical power (which can be used to generate electricity). The most common types of solar thermal devices being commercially produced today are flat-plate hot-water collectors, used for simple hot-water heating. More advanced thermal collectors, those using systems of concentrating collectors or mirrors to produce mechanical energy, are still being researched and produced on a very small scale.

[b]Biogas is one method of recovering energy from organic materials. It is produced by anaerobic digestion—a fermenting process performed by a mixture of micro-organisms in the absence of oxygen. Biogas generators convert cow dung, human excrement, and inedible agricultural residues into a mixture of methane and carbon dioxide that can be burnt as a fuel. The liquid residue left after biogasification is a rich fertilizer that retains all the original nutrients of the wastes.

provide AID with the knowledge on which to base sound project ideas and fit them into a well-conceived energy planning effort. The challenge is to gather behind both approaches the momentum, conviction, and funding needed to make an appreciable difference.

The differences in approach of these two aid programs in Mali also point to one of the significant barriers to improving energy supply and use in the Third World. A false perception of choices frequently springs from the view that one type of energy is more, or less, appropriate to developing world needs. Thus there are advocates of nuclear power, of solar energy, of biomass,^{c} of hydrogen fuel. These advocates concentrate on energy technologies rather than on the needs that energy fills. This narrowness becomes even more troublesome because of the often made, but simplistic, assumption that financial resources are somehow fungible, or transferable from expenditures on one type of energy technology to another. For example, the EDF's program in Mali is spending large sums on the most sophisticated (and expensive) form of solar energy, photovoltaic cells. It could be argued that these funds might be better spent on firewood projects. This might *ideally* be true, but in fact the money is only available because this type of project promotes an expanding European solar energy industry, which needs subsidized markets to get off the ground. Indeed, the Malian example shows clearly by just how much professional opinions can differ on focusing effort and allocating investment.

This chapter is concerned with this problem of targetry. It examines present attitudes toward the availability of, and the problems with, some energy sources for which there are substantial expectations in the Third World. We do not discuss all the energy sources available for developing country application. Rather, we concentrate on the most likely prospects for the converged efforts of the industrial North, Third World oil importers, and OPEC, which we believe to be practical possibilities. Because our focus is North-South cooperation, we concentrate on the technologies and energy sources that are most susceptible to transfer. For example, we pay little attention here to the potential for biomass fuels, even though they are surely one of the most promising options for quite a few developing countries, because biomass programs involve relatively small capital investment and no transfer of sophisticated technology from North to South. Biomass programs can largely be carried out by

^{c}Biomass is a general term referring to all those processes which seek to recover energy directly from plant matter. Biomass (or photosynthetic fuel) processes can be designed to produce solids (wood and charcoal), liquids (oils and alcohols), gases (methane and hydrogen), or electricity.

Third World countries on their own, without foreign help (although there is probably a great deal of scope for technical cooperation *among* developing countries).

What, then, are the energy sources available to Third World countries with which Western help and advice is most likely to make a difference? We start with the energy source whose shortage has captured the world's attention.

OIL

There have never been significant efforts to develop fossil fuel resources in the majority of the developing countries. In 1975 over 40,000 wells were drilled in the United States and Canada. During that same year less than 4,500 were drilled in the non-OPEC Third World. If oil is not looked for, it certainly will not be found.[d] The reasons for this state of affairs are discussed below, but first it is important to survey the conditions that dominate oil use in many developing countries.

Both the international and the local purchase of oil are subsidized directly or indirectly in most developing countries. Oil-importing developing countries (OIDCs) buy oil on international credit that they cannot hope to repay in the foreseeable future. And within many of these countries, consumer purchase of oil products, particularly kerosene, is also subsidized by the national government. The reason for this state of affairs says much about the Third World outlook on oil demand. In developed countries it is increasingly accepted that we are approaching the *end* of the oil era.[e] But many developing countries—at least the majority of the populations of many countries who before 1973 had begun to anticipate the amenities of cheap energy in their lives—have barely entered the oil era. Their transition into petroleum-based economies has been slowed dramatically, and now the question remains whether pricing policies and other incentives can be rethought quickly enough to make it feasible to avoid heavy oil dependence wherever possible.

[d]A step in the right direction is the World Bank's new oil-gas program. See infra pp. 72-75 and Appendix 3, p. 131.

[e]In fact, however, this is a great oversimplification of the situation, based on extrapolations of rates of *growth* of oil consumption. By contrast, it has recently been calculated (see Bonn International Conference Energy Resources Working Group, "Agricultural Production: Research and Development Strategies for the 1980s," Conference Document, 1979) that if the North cuts its oil consumption by 15 percent by the year 2000, the oil consumption of the South could grow simultaneously at 5-6 percent—and in the year 2000, on present proven reserves, there would still be sixty years' supply of oil left.

In practice, the imperatives of immediate need are arrayed against these long-range pressures, particularly because oil supply and price projections have always underestimated the impact of political events. (Of eight prominent oil forecasts conducted between 1975 and 1978, only one, the Workshop on Alternative Energy Strategies, suggested that OPEC might impose political limits on *production*. And none of the major forecasts looked ahead to the Iranian crisis and its effects on world oil supply.)[f] Not only are OIDCs faced with additional threats over the next ten years, but they also suffer most in times of crisis. Some of the poorest countries cannot meet their minimal needs when world demand soars, and the spot markets are often unavailable to them simply because of their lack of ready cash.

On top of this, the Third World is not organized to allocate oil among its needy countries, a problem that the North attempted to solve for itself by creating the International Energy Agency. While distribution of OPEC oil is still carried out largely by major international oil companies, since 1975 many smaller-scale buyers (such as refineries, traders, and even a few countries) have dealt directly with OPEC producers. But still most of the poorer countries have almost no protection against being passed altogether by tankers headed for Northern ports, although in mid-1979, Saudi Arabia claimed to have earmarked a small production increase for sale exclusively in OIDCs, at the established Saudi price. Finally, oil prices in many areas of the Third World, particularly rural areas, are often several times those of the United States or Europe. Transport costs are higher due to inadequate ports and roads and this can double or triple the effective price of a barrel.

The scale of recent discoveries in Mexico highlighted the potential for fossil fuel recovery in some developing countries. But although the entry of a potential major exporter into the world market has great importance for major consuming countries, the more significant breakthrough may be the recovery of previously unexploited or undiscovered reserves for domestic use on a comparatively small scale. The World Bank estimates that as many as thirty-eight oil-importing countries have reserves sufficient to make a very significant difference in the availability of oil for their own domestic consumption.[1] Why have

[f]These forecasts were by (1) U.S. Central Intelligence Agency, (2) U.S. Department of Energy (1978), (3) U.S. Energy Information Agency (1978), (4) Brookhaven National Laboratory (U.S.) (1978), (5) International Energy Agency (OECD) (1978), (6) Rockefeller Foundation (1978), (7) Workshop on Alternative Energy Strategies (1977), (8) Petroleum Industry Research Foundation (1977).

these reserves not been developed in the past? One of the main reasons is that international oil companies have had little incentive to carry out the expensive exploratory operations that precede production. In Africa, for example, this can be attributed both to political circumstances (a general wariness of political instability and possible nationalization) and to geography (oil produced away from the coast is difficult and expensive to transport). In Latin America, on the other hand, countries with known reserves have been extremely protective of their development, and in some cases unsophisticated in the complicated international negotiations that lead to production. Peru, for example, may have substantial undeveloped reserves in its northern areas. In the early seventies, concessions were leased to a dozen or so major oil companies. But the government imposed such unpalatable restrictions—such as harsh financial penalties for insufficient exploratory drilling—that most of the companies faced an absurd choice. If preparatory work dictated a halt to operations, they either had to pay large fines or drill redundant wells in difficult, largely jungle, conditions. When the U.S. Internal Revenue Service allowed the option of writing off these losses against income, most of the companies gave up. Only recently, the one company that stayed on has made major discoveries, and others may now be attracted to return. But five years' delay is probably costing Peru millions of dollars in lost foreign exchange spent for imported oil.

Oil exploration is a risky business. Major companies usually try to spread the risk among entrepreneurs and subcontractors. But in the case of the poorest countries, this has been impossible because of the absence of the financial and managerial capability needed to plan for and direct exploration. Another significant blockage to oil development in the Third World can be traced to domestic political priorities. In Turkey, for example, the price of oil at the wellhead has been tightly controlled in order to subsidize domestic prices for consumers (a policy that has recently been changing). In addition, the Turkish National Oil Company has held all the best concessions for years. These two conditions have totally blocked any serious international exploration or production activity, despite the fact that Turkey spends more on imported oil than it earns from all of its national exports combined.

Of course, the greatest deterrent has been that the international price fetched before 1973 made small-scale deposits in remote locations entirely noncompetitive, and so even known deposits were usually left in the ground by the major oil companies. In theory, a developing country could hire exploration services, buy equipment, and contract for technical services to develop its oil resources. But in practice, the challenges of such an undertaking have, till now, proved insurmountable. The advantage held by the major companies is not that they have exclusive control over oil recovery technology. Rather, their advantage has lain in concentrating on management, knowledge, capacity to hire skills, and marketing networks: capacities that give them the ability to organize and coordinate huge and integrated technical and financial operations. Now, however, the present and prospective price of oil may offer remarkable opportunities for creative entrepreneurship in mobilizing national or regional enterprises for the exploration of small oil deposits.

ELECTRICITY

The benefits of electricity need hardly be reiterated. Unfortunately, there are two principal limitations on the contribution of electricity to development: cost and access. Electricity is already far too expensive to be purchased by the truly needy. It has been estimated that the costs of new electrical generating and transmission capacity to supply the equivalent of one daily barrel of oil are $37,000 for electricity produced from fossil fuel and $46,000 for nuclear or hydroelectricity.[2] In 1977 electricity prices in developing countries were two to four times typical consumer prices in the U.S. and Europe.[3] Despite these difficulties, electrification in both the city and the countryside is, ordinarily, a priority goal of almost all Third World countries. Three large-scale sources of electricity are available: hydroelectric, fossil fuel, and nuclear.

Hydropower

Although oil dominates the commercial energy market in the Third World, hydroelectric power projects have long known favor with development financing agencies. Many great dams were planned and built during the 1960s, but before the oil embargo most of the obvious locations for large-scale projects, near population and industrial centers, had been developed. The oil price rises of the 1970s have changed the economics of hydroelectric power drastically, so that higher transmission costs from remote river basins have become justifiable. A renewed interest in hydropower has surfaced in the last three years, although the lead times and construction period for hydroelectric dams are long, so that the impact has not yet been fully felt.

Changing attitudes toward rural development must, however, be taken into account in examining potential cost advantages for hydroelectric development. In the last few years the concept of "integrated" rural development has come into wide currency with both developing country governments and aid agencies. Such integrated development planning reflects a new level of concern for the broad social and environmental consequences of development. For example, in some development assistance agencies (for example, the Regional Development Program of the Organization of American States) planners now look for the most desirable development opportunities in a river basin, rather than simply assuming that a large dam is the best alternative.

However, with the return to favor of hydroelectric power, there is the danger that environmental consequences will once again be overlooked under countervailing economic considerations. This is true despite the fact that environmental factors such as heavy siltation of a reservoir have, in the past, ruined major projects, literally undermining the initial investment. In fact, major dam schemes are currently under construction in Africa and elsewhere that ignore almost every lesson that should have been learned from the environmental disasters associated with the large dams of the 1960s.[4] Decisions to plan and finance many more large dams reflect the habitual methods of major construction and engineering projects in the Western industrialized countries more than they reflect fresh analysis of the real needs of developing country populations. This in part explains why, despite a good deal of talk, so little serious attention has been given to the prospects for small hydroelectric projects. Exploitation of the remaining potential for hydroelectric production will be subjected to delay roughly in proportion to the scale of the project (due to the heavy initial capital costs and the time and organizational skills required to prepare a hydroelectric plan for financing). Moreover, as the best remaining sites for large schemes are located in mountainous areas, generally far from population centers, transmission costs will tend to show smaller hydro schemes to further advantage.

Of course, the development of more small hydroelectric projects will by no means negate the need for the development of larger dams (which are, at least, a renewable energy source). Larger hydroelectric facilities will continue to be competitive for industrial, urban markets, and potentially very valuable as the centerpiece of the integrated agricultural and industrial development, for example, of a river basin region. However, smaller markets and isolated rural areas can be served by smaller dams. There are myriad sites in developing countries suitable for medium to very small hydro installations. In a brief review of the distribution of population in Tanzania, it was reported that a surprisingly large proportion of Tanzanians live close to year-round streams.[5] Tanzania is generally dry country, so it is not unreasonable to suppose the same findings are likely to be true of some other developing countries with the same conditions.

It should not be imagined, however, that small-scale hydro or other water-control projects need less in the way of careful environmental attention than large barrages. Jamaica, for example, has a program for building over 200 microdams for mini-hydropower generation and irrigation. Five of the six built in the project's initial plan failed to hold water because the bedrock of the valley, which was limestone, had been insufficiently surveyed, and the floodwater simply disappeared into the porous rock. The Chinese, on the other hand, have been able to provide most of the electricity for three-quarters of their rural communes with mini-hydro generators,[6] and there seems no reason why many developing countries should not, despite having far weaker cooperative systems than China, achieve far more than is even contemplated at present.

Coal

Unlike much of the developed world, which largely shifted its energy dependence from coal to oil in the fifties and sixties, the developing world has always generated most of its electricity with oil-fired power plants. With the continuing rise in oil prices, however, prospects for widespread coal use seem to be on the rise. It is cause for some concern that this is true in spite of widespread warnings in the scientific community over the probable impact of increased coal use on the atmosphere and the world's climate (through increased carbon dioxide emission and the spread of "acid rain"). Most experts agree that these issues call for careful scrutiny. Many are convinced, nonetheless, that coal is the best available "transitional" fuel; that is, coal could be used in place of oil while replacement energy sources are developed and applied worldwide.[7]

It certainly looks as if enough coal is *physically* available to accomplish this task (although coal may be distributed even more unevenly than oil). Known world coal reserves are about five times as large as known oil reserves. Most of these *known* reserves are found in the United States, the Soviet Union, and China (only 3 percent of presently known coal deposits are in developing countries). In the developing world, only India has large known reserves, though Botswana, Brazil, Indonesia, and Swaziland are also thought to have substantial coal deposits. Even compared to oil, very little of this coal in the Third World is mined and used. India mines significant amounts of it, but is joined only by Yugoslavia, the Republic of Korea, and Turkey.[8]

Very little is really known about the potential for coal production in the Third World, primarily because there has been almost no exploration for coal and, as with oil, most developing countries lack sufficiently detailed geological data. No worldwide rush has developed to locate and mine coal deposits in Third World countries, although coal is still much cheaper than oil (particularly when compared in terms of the value of heat content). This situation prevails both because private companies have not been attracted by coal's price, and also because coal is more difficult and expensive to transport than oil. This leaves aside the tantalizing question, of course, whether the United States or the Soviet Union could become major coal exporters to the Third World. That development has not begun to happen, in part because a large capital investment would be needed to switch to coal use in developing countries. Coal-fired power plants would, however, meet developing country needs for reliability and flexibility in size (they can be easily adapted to growing electricity demand without disrupting the entire distribution system). In short, the changing politics and price of oil make almost every eventuality seem within the bounds of possibility.

It would be very difficult to promote the expanded development of coal in Third World countries at the moment, because the demand to buy the coal does not exist. The World Bank has conducted one of the few reviews of constraints to coal use and concluded that a large effort would be needed to promote longer range energy planning (thus allowing for the long lead times to develop coal resources) and to create the needed institutional and technical expertise, which is now almost totally missing. Finally, unlike the expanded use of some other fuels, enlarged interest in coal in the Third World may depend, in great part, on trends in the developed countries. Without an assured demand for coal (perhaps in Western Europe or Japan), there will be no export opportunities, and without research and development work in the North, there are unlikely to be any technical innovations that would be applicable in developing countries.

Nuclear Power

In the early 1970s hopes for nuclear energy as a potential source of electric power in developing countries were very great. The International Atomic Energy Agency (IAEA) published *A Market Survey for Nuclear Power in Developing Countries* in 1974, which estimated that 140 reactors could be sold to Third World countries in the years 1981-1989. In May 1976 the IEA halved that estimate, and six months later officials were privately admitting that the estimate had been quartered.

Commercial nuclear power stations are operating in only six developing countries today, and in most respects nuclear power is ill suited to the foreseeable needs of almost all developing countries. Nuclear plants smaller than 200 megawatts are simply not available, yet very few developing countries have national electric grids that can accommodate plants larger than 200 megawatts, because stable electricity distribution requires that no more than 15 percent of the power come from any one generating station. Nuclear power plant construction is one of the most capital-intensive undertakings in the world today, and the return on investment lies years in the future.

The most glaring flaw in Northern efforts to promote nuclear power for the Third World has been pointed out with increasing frequency by developing country analysts and officials. In the short run, the nuclear industry fosters nearly total reliance on developed country technology. Most developing countries are now plagued by large balance of payments deficits, and they fear the political ramifications of external reliance for energy supply, yet virtually all of the equipment and the fuel for nuclear power must be imported, even by nations with indigenous uranium resources. In Iran, for example, even cement had to be imported from Germany because no cement manufacturer in Iran could provide materials that met minimum stress standards for safety purposes. A few of the most scientifically advanced developing countries, like Argentina, India, and Brazil, have advancing nuclear programs based on local capabilities. But it is, nevertheless, quite clear that the immense export subsidy programs available to nuclear plant manufacturers have been designed without particular regard to the needs or the financial predicament of much of the potential "market."

Electricity Distribution

While controversy has raged over the cost, availability, and safety of oil and atomic-powered electricity generation, an issue with farther-reaching consequences has been left relatively unexamined.[9] The distribution of electric power within most developing countries tends to reinforce existing inequalities. Rural access to centrally generated electricity is still negligible in many areas. Only about 4 percent of rural Africans, and 23 percent of rural Latin Americans are able to have electricity.[10] Thus, although most developing countries have become genuinely alarmed at the migration of rural populations to the cities, their energy distribution policies continue to encourage this trend. The proclivities of most development aid agencies do not provide a countering influence, since generation and distribution projects continue to consume roughly one-quarter of most aid budgets.

Electrical power can be provided to potential rural consumers, if it is found to be desirable compared to other energy options, in one of three ways: Central station electrical grids could be extended to reach them; small, decentralized generators using conventional fuels could be installed; or electrical systems using locally available renewable resources could be installed. As of 1975 over 80 percent of rural electricity was supplied from central station grids,[11] for which the capital costs are much higher than for decentralized systems. The decentralized approaches improve access but may dramatically increase operating and maintenance costs. When the system is heavily utilized, the capital-intensive centralized approach is strongly favored over the fuel-intensive, decentralized approach. Moreover, once a grid is in place, the marginal costs of expanding service to nearby centers of demand are often relatively low. Indeed, such expansion may lower system-wide unit costs, thus serving as strong stimulus for increasing the generating capacity.

The cost-comparisons are reversed, however, for service areas remote from existing networks, due to the large costs of transmission links and "line-losses" of electricity. We are not arguing that rural electrification programs should be discontinued. But transmission lines are now so expensive (in 1976 a 400-kw line cost more than $80,000 per mile) that it is questionable in a number of cases whether the benefits of rural electrification would survive the rigorous economic analysis to which the benefits of decentralized, renewable energy sources are now subjected.[12]

Centrally based power projects are, of course, essential for modern industrial growth, but most aid agency commitments to rural electrification programs have not been reconsidered. In part, this is attributable to the political importance of pledges to electrify rural areas, which are essential to successful politics in many Third World countries. Although the commitment to meeting "basic human needs" has gradually spread as official policy throughout the national and international agencies, the situation in India is not atypical. The electricity that reaches villages there is rarely purchased by more than 20 percent of the households, which means that far fewer than 20 percent of the residents receive its benefits, since wealthier families tend to be smaller than poorer families.[13] In these circumstances, the future of traditional approaches to rural electrification, long considered so vital to agricultural productivity, has come under increasing challenge. However, commitment to alternatives has not taken hold.

SOLAR ENERGY

Much has been promised for the "technologies of the future," most of which take energy more or less directly from the sun. Is solar energy a practical solution to the energy problems of the Third World? The question is not easily answered, particularly because it is often misconstrued, but interest in the possibilities of solar energy is growing extremely rapidly in North and South alike. The Tata Energy Research Institute in India has conducted a survey that found more than sixty-three countries and nine international organizations carrying out solar research and development programs.[g] During the fiscal year 1979, the U.S. Department of Energy spent $500 million on solar research and increased that amount by about 50 percent in 1980. The world's second biggest solar spender, France, allocated over 260 million francs ($62 million) in 1978 to solar research and development. Finally, investment in solar energy now looks sufficiently attractive that the interest of major international companies, particularly the oil industry, has recently been awakened, so that many small solar companies have been acquired by much larger firms.

Certain solar energy applications for developing countries have already failed to meet the hopes of their promoters. Continuous efforts with solar cookers in West Africa and elsewhere have never really taken hold. The technology was unfamiliar, it was not possible to design it for use within existing lifestyles (cooking had to take place at an unpopular time of day and at an unaccustomed slow rate), and as a result the experiment is now generally regarded as a failure. Likewise, a French solar hot-plate company made an early effort to distribute irrigation pumps powered by solar thermal collectors through the French aid program in the Sahel and in Mexico. The problems with this heat-collecting device have been severe, particularly because the motors driven by the solar heat often break down under tough rural conditions. The director of the Latin American Office of the United Nations Environment Programme said of the Mexican project that it had been "very profitable for the French and costly to the Mexicans. It does not generate employment; there is increasing dependency on foreign technologies; it is capital-intensive; and contrary to the long life expected, in less than five years of operation, out of thirteen plants, only one is in operation."[14]

Expectations about solar energy derive almost entirely from how one perceives its eventual applications. In the United States, for example, the President's Council on Environmental Quality had predicted that solar energy could provide up to 25 percent of America's energy needs by the year 2000.[15] The U.S. Department of Energy vigorously disagreed, arguing that a realistic figure would be closer to 8 percent, but American policy has adopted the higher figure,

[g]See Table 2 for a summary of solar research and development being carried out in the Third World.

since President Carter publicly stated a target of 20 percent.[16] The debate is important because it influences the type of research and development that is carried out in developed countries. The DOE program's emphasis, in the view of an increasingly respected body of critics, is badly misplaced:

> Far too much of the present research program is directed at "big solar," expensive high technology projects that mimic the space and nuclear programs. There are two prominent examples. One is the power tower, which would use acres of mirrors to focus light in order to heat water to boiling; it accounts for a fifth of the government's entire solar research and development budget. The other is the orbiting satellite, which would beam the sun's energy back to earth, and whose supporters have attempted to obtain large-scale funding.[17]

This approach ignores a fundamental characteristic of solar energy: that it is available everywhere, and that there are few economies of scale in centralizing its generation, as compared to the economic necessity of centralizing conventional power generation. If the costs of storing solar electricity can be reduced, solar power generating units may greatly lower the delivered cost of electricity by eliminating or reducing transmission costs.

Northern disagreement over the best way to develop solar energy has three consequences for potential use in the Third World. First, it means that the debate over solar energy centers on the question, "When will solar electricity be competitive with other sources?" That question, and much of the analysis that pursues it, tends to assume that competing sources of energy are *available* or *affordable*, and that they will continue to be available in the future. For example, animal muscle power to pump water may be the only alternative to solar pumps. But one must consider the environmental (as well as economic) costs of keeping the necessary cattle at work. Where fuelwood is almost exhausted, one must also consider the environmental and economic costs of burning dung instead of using it for fertilizer, and so forth. Likewise, extensions from electricity grids are only prohibitively costly in rural Third World areas if one assumes minimal consumption targets, but if one does not assume minimal consumption targets, one ignores the relative poverty of the potential purchasers and the small amounts of electrical energy they may actually demand.

This leads to the second misconception that has been fostered. Sometimes costs appear exorbitant because of the level of energy use that is assumed. For example, running a flashlight on dry-cell batteries is extremely expensive in "dollars per watt," but is in fact tolerably cheap because only a couple of watts are used and flashlights are very useful for certain specific purposes. In the same way, water from solar-powered irrigation pumps may be "expensive" today, but this expense may be justified as an investment in research and development, in the same way that billions of dollars were spent on nuclear research technology over nearly two decades before the first commercially viable reactor was linked to an electricity grid. There may be no alternative to solar-powered irrigation for the foreseeable future that is in fact affordable and available for meeting minimal water needs in remote areas. Innovative demonstration and application techniques of reliable equipment are probably needed, then, more than further technological breakthroughs, provided one is searching for available solutions to today's energy problems.

Third, solar energy projects are evaluated with methods that are deficient with respect to Third World use. Traditional economic cost-benefit analysis assigns a value only to benefits for which a direct monetary value can be calculated. But the application of a solar energy technology in a remote area should not be compared simply to its theoretical competition, but to its *actual* competition. Thus, it should be a substantial "benefit" that energy will be available where it would not have been for some time to come if other sources were awaited. Another gap in the present system is the absence of field testing set up to enable adaptation of new technologies in light of local resources, activities, and energy needs. Products intended to use solar energy technology—both power sources themselves or solar-powered products (for example, refrigerators)—have not been designed for local conditions in poor countries. This causes good opportunities to be missed. For example, an important opportunity for international solar marketing today is in hot-water heaters for the rich in tropical and semitropical countries—including the tourist industry. Not only would rich consumers benefit, but conventional fuel consumption and hence all imports would of course be reduced. The new systems would be emulated within countries as fast as the middle class could afford it. Furthermore, the wealthy in poor countries own most industries; the sooner they become familiar with domestic solar benefits, the sooner they will start adapting their manufacturing.

A final problem can be traced to the difficulties encountered by large institutions such as aid agencies in recognizing and seizing opportunities that require deviation from "business as usual." A few solar technologies for a few applications are competitive today in certain areas of the Third World where all the circumstances are right. And if the cost of photovoltaic cells drops as much by 1985 as is now widely predicted, the opportunities may increase and diversify dramatically.[h] Examples of project opportunities are discussed in Chapter 4. Once photovoltaic cells begin to enter the energy market, their toehold becomes an economic force that reduces the price of the cells (through increased production), and thus accelerates continued expansion of the market and continued reduction in price. The vexing problem is locating purchasing power that will unleash this cycle.

To summarize, many observers believe that there is a large potential market for solar energy technology in the Third World. Others are sceptical and stress that a market cannot exist among poor people who have no funds to pay for energy. Not only solar energy but renewable energy sources in general tend to be burdened by excessive optimism and excessive suspicion arising from these opposed points of view. Optimism in some developing countries derives from an uncritical faith in the imperative of technological advance; if a problem exists, modernizing technology will provide a solution. Yet at the same time, no belief is more bitterly debated in the Third World, carrying as it inevitably must, the specter of continuing dependence on the North.

Developed country optimists for solar prospects in the Third World (especially, of course, the manufacturers) generally tend to underestimate the nontechnical barriers to the technology's workability that have to be overcome. Not surprisingly, this naiveté is not much found in the majority of aid agencies. Indeed, suspicions over the applicability of the new energy technologies in developing countries tend mainly to follow from the view that technologies unproven in developed countries should not be subsidized in, or sold to, developing countries. Yet this scepticism contains its own danger. An important lesson of thirty years of development aid has been that proven success of a technology in a *developed* country tells very little about its probable success in a *developing* country.

There is, again, no simple and obvious way ahead. But fortunately, a small but vocal minority of developers has come to advocate design, testing, demonstration, and adaptation in the region where energy technologies will be used. A substantial commitment to this process might go a long way toward dispelling another Third World

[h]The price of photovoltaic cells is measured in peak watts, one of which is the output of a solar electric cell under the best possible conditions—noon on a sunny day. In 1979 a peak watt cost between $10 and $12 dollars; the 1985 price is predicted to be fifty cents.

suspicion—that developing countries are to be the proving ground of the North's future energy sources. This suspicion, as will be seen in Chapter 4, is not entirely unfounded.

FIREWOOD

The other energy sources discussed in this chapter are primarily available to people who pay for the energy they consume. Firewood and other traditional fuels such as cow dung, on the other hand, have been freely available, historically, to poor people in most areas of the world. But now firewood is running short. It has become an expensive commercial commodity, and its growing shortage is the single greatest contribution to a new worldwide problem: Poor people's access to their traditional energy sources is increasingly limited by supply, distance, and cost.

Although it is increasingly common to speak of a *world* firewood crisis, the depletion and rising cost of fuelwood actually center in three types of geographic regions. On the fringes of arid savannah lands, generally far away from concentrated timber supplies, the shortage of fuelwood is desperate. In these areas, wood gatherers often cut any newly planted trees that are accessible. In the mountainous areas of Latin America, Central Africa, and particularly South Asia, the planting of trees and bushes for fuelwood, fodder, and erosion control is needed urgently. And in highly populated areas, often near growing cities, there is too little wood to meet the constantly rising demand of fast-growing populations. In a fourth geographic region—the agricultural frontier in the humid tropics, where countries are seeking alternatives to the traditional slash-and-burn method of clearing new agricultural areas where tropical forests once stood—forest loss will eventually lead to firewood shortages as populations move in and increase.

It is no simple task to categorize all the direct and side effects of this situation. Certainly desertification—the loss of once fertile soil—is a direct result. Soils deteriorate, and water supplies become unmanageable in concert with growing problems of erosion. The rapid depletion of the world's forest cover is probably not caused directly by scavenging for firewood, but the building pressure on forests is exacerbated by the need for wood, particularly as the price of wood and charcoal inflates in cities not too distant from forests.

In these circumstances, it is important to remember that people who use firewood use it because they have no other choice. In the cities, however, the high cost of wood fuel now means that it may be compared to possible substitutes. Despite increased oil prices, people in some areas of countries like Kenya are still substituting kerosene for wood in *increasing* numbers. To face the long-range problems, particularly for rural use, increasing amounts of land need to be devoted to growing trees. But serious conflicts will soon arise between devoting land to growing wood and devoting land to growing food. Again in Kenya, one-third of the land at most is cultivable for food, so there are doubts about the possibility of turning any of it over to forestry. And many countries are far less fertile than Kenya. One solution might be to plant forests on land that is considered noncultivable for agriculture, although populations tend not to locate in these areas as heavily as elsewhere, and the soil would be sufficiently fertile only in rare cases.

In the face of these problems, the best solutions may be those that enhance management of traditional fuels—for example, by promoting more efficient burning of wood and charcoal or improved production of fuel from existing wood resources.[18] Increasing hopes center around the results that might be achieved by introducing more efficient stove designs. Cooking over an open fire achieves no better than 10 percent fuel use efficiency, probably worse, and most traditional stoves do not do much better. Several practical and ultralow-cost new stove designs are now, however, available. Some use entirely local materials, such as clay; others use such implements as discarded oil drums and can be assembled with simple tools. In both cases, firewood consumption can reportedly be cut by as much as 50 percent compared to use in open fires, and stoves generally have the added health advantage of carrying smoke out of the house.

The technology of more efficient wood and charcoal burning stoves is quite simple.[19] The problem is not technological, but involves the need to demonstrate the stoves' value and effectiveness to potential users and to train local craftsmen to build and install them. The World Bank will apparently in future devote a very modest percentage of most forestry projects to the creation of small-scale, local stove-building industries. The idea would probably involve training craftsmen, who then would become the local entrepreneurs of the stove industry. Materials for most of the new stoves cost less than five dollars, so that if the price for the user can be kept under ten dollars, in urban areas a stove would pay for itself in reduced fuelwood expenditure in less than one year. This would be an attractive investment for all but the very poorest villagers and urban dwellers.

Is it also possible to increase the total available *supply* of firewood? Large wood plantations are appearing in many countries, but the problems associated with these efforts—and the scale needed to achieve meaningful results—are immense. The Asian Development Bank, for example, estimates that reforestation in Asian developing countries would have to be expanded to a rate of 10 million hectares (24.8 million acres) per year, at an annual cost of $400–800 million, in order to avoid a wood deficit in 1990 of 170 million m^3.[i]

The need is at least as great in Africa. Kenya probably needs to plant close to 10 million acres of trees between now and the year 2000 to keep up with firewood demands. The government is committed to planting trees on large plantations, and it will also encourage farmers and villagers to establish small woodlots for local consumption. This approach can ideally have the important advantage that village inhabitants will see the direct benefits they obtain from protecting and caring for the young trees, although it is difficult to get such projects started. The record of failed attempts of some similar efforts points to the need for a reorientation of forestry services toward cooperation with villagers and training for land and plant management.

There have already been successful programs that have gone far toward solving national fuelwood problems. In the early 1970s the Republic of Korea introduced a national reforestation scheme that was in part based on village woodlots and farmed on village land. It also undertook a national publicity campaign to alert rural inhabitants about the danger to forest cover and to persuade them to take full advantage of available ways of conserving fuel. Firewood shortages have, as a result, been substantially reduced. But an even more encouraging example may be found in Gujarat state, in India, which lacked the initial Korean advantage of a highly cooperative society. Gujarat began to face its wood and fuel shortage in 1969 by establishing plantations along roads and canals (nearby communities share the profits). Later, Gujarat officials added a village planting program, supplying seedlings and paying villagers to plant them. The autocratic *panchayats*, or town councils, share profits with the state forest department.[20]

Is there a role for Northern aid in the massive reforestation effort that is so badly needed? We believe there is, both to stimulate interest and to provide the technical and social skills and the money needed to emulate successes like those of South Korea and Gujarat.

[i]See Peter H. Freeman, "Forestry in Development Assistance," (prepared for U.S. Agency for International Development, September 1979). Freeman provides information assembled from World Bank sources that shows the scale of effort needed to meet the wood supply problem. (See Table 3.) For fifteen selected countries, tree planting would have to be increased by factors ranging *from four to fifty*, and this generously assumes a large degree of wood replacement by other renewable energy sources.

And finally, of course, if aid programs are intended to alleviate poverty, Northern governments cannot overlook this opportunity to focus a greater part of their energy aid on programs that benefit those who have no access to electricity, and who could not afford it if they did.

CONSERVATION AND PRODUCTIVITY

Concern over firewood shortages and the intense interest generated by the future for solar energy technologies may well divert attention from the improvement of efficiency in the use of present energy sources. More than one official has expressed the fear that unwarranted confidence in the arrival of renewable energy technologies may cause government planners to ignore immediate opportunities, such as improved energy efficiency in the agricultural sector.

Indeed, it may be that the practical difficulties and the costs associated with the transfer of alternative energy technologies to the rural Third World, together with the rate of Third World urbanization and the relative scale of energy use involved, combine to establish energy conservation in cities as the first priority in a number of Third World countries. This topic has been politically charged for some time, because the rhetorical response until quite recently has been that energy conservation is "antidevelopment." The truth of the matter is that any energy saved saves scarce funds that can be spent elsewhere. Increasing the productivity and efficiency with which fuel is used, in both the rural and urban Third World, should be far higher on the agendas of international institutions and developing country ministries than it has been to date.

Project designers need not look far to find opportunities to follow this approach, as our discussion of firewood programs indicated. One example is an agricultural project in the Cameroons that the World Bank began funding in 1971. Electricity for irrigation and milling was originally generated from diesel fuel, but recently the Bank funded a small study to investigate adapting the generators to burn agricultural waste products. Twenty-five percent of the local rice harvest is husk, which up to now has been wasted, but in future it could be burned to produce enough electricity to provide for all the needs of the project and for local residents as well. Many energy specialists believe there is almost no reason why an agro-industrial project cannot now be energy self-sufficient, and even productive, in this way. One area for immediate attention is the sugar-milling industry, a field in which the United Nations Industrial Development Organization (UNIDO) has recently shown great interest.

The problems with persuading energy users to adapt their habits to the recycling of otherwise discarded materials are as great in the South as they are in the North. The most notable example has been the disappointments associated with the national biogas program initiated by India. In theory, small-scale decentralized biogas plants could provide energy at village level. In practice, however, the program has met severe problems: Families that owned fewer than three or four cattle could not afford to own a plant independently; yet, for social and cultural reasons, cooperative buying proved nearly impossible. In addition, the collection of dung meant that fertilizer became less widely available, and also that a commercial value became attached to a fuel that had previously been free to any of the poor who took time to gather it.

But the greatest opportunities for saving energy in the Third World—and the area where there is surely the most room for the North to help—are to be found in the modern (industrial and transportation) sectors, which are typically even more dependent in Third World countries upon imported oil than in the United States and Europe. And, as in the Northern industrial nations, the fastest, cheapest, and cleanest potential source of new oil is more productive use of existing sources. Not remarkably, patterns of commercial energy production and use in developing countries have tended to emulate those of developed countries, often because energy conversion technologies, construction techniques, manufacturing processes, and energy-using equipment have been transferred wholesale. So too, improvements in such technologies and processes can be transferred through development assistance programs. Compounding the inefficiencies of imported technologies have been the endemic ones associated with rapid urbanization and the increasing energy intensity of the privileged social classes. Human settlement patterns in the developing countries as a whole rely heavily upon food, construction, and transport systems that are energy-intensive and thus promote wasteful use of energy.

THE LIMITS TO
TECHNOLOGICAL SOLUTIONS

Clearly no one energy source or technology will be right for every developing country, any more than this would be the case for an industrialized country. But aid-giving countries face a special problem in advising developing countries on how best to achieve the correct "mix" of energy sources for their particular circumstances because it can be extremely difficult to suspend developed country biases in offering this advice. It is rarely true that technological choices are obvious; it is simply that the biases or values of whoever is choosing are pronounced.

For example, sharpening the focus of publicly financed programs must start with clear definitions of the target populations to be reached and of levels of improvement to be aimed at. A study of solar energy application in Tanzania led to the broad conclusion that each of five small-scale solar technologies that were studied was able to compete with diesel generators or extensions from the electric grid, or would be able to do so within a few years.[21] These conclusions have been criticized because the study assumed that the villagers would consume quite low levels of energy (1 kwh per person per day). Would energy projects modeled on this and similar studies have a big enough impact, and soon enough, to make village life more attractive to villagers? The criticism of the Tanzanian study implied that legitimate Third World aspirations for more energy-intensive lives were not being taken seriously. These criticisms may well be valid if one has resources adequate to provide comprehensive help to a region or country as a whole. *But if available funds are limited, as they inevitably will be, then a developing country government must choose:* Will it try to have an incremental effect on the lives of many villages, or a startling impact on the lives of a few?

As these judgments are made, developed countries must take care not to impose their own perceptions of energy planning on developing countries. Few Third World countries have either the knowledge or the management skills and planning capacities to devise an energy strategy that mobilizes an appropriate mix of alternatives. It has therefore become conventional wisdom that developing countries need better data on their energy supply and demand, better information about the energy uses of the population, more sophisticated management structures and planning capabilities, and probably more sophisticated research capability. *The point is rarely made that all of these needs are endemic to a total condition of underdevelopment, and that real progress cannot be achieved in one area significantly beyond progress in others.* And so, though policymakers must establish alternatives among technological approaches, they must also establish priorities among the range of institutional support and planning activities that are possible. Both types of priorities should reflect the wide variation in sophistication among developing country energy needs and energy planning. If they do not, past habitual mistakes of North-South transfers will make an unscheduled, disastrous reappearance.

NOTES

1. World Bank, *A Program to Accelerate Petroleum Production in the Developing Countries* (Washington, D.C.: World Bank, 1979), p. 17.

2. Philip F. Palmedo, et al., *Energy Needs, Uses and Resources in Developing Countries* (Upton, N.Y.: Brookhaven National Laboratory, March 1978), Table B19, p. 57.

3. Office of Technology Assessment, *Applications of Solar Technology to Today's Energy Needs*, vol. 1 (Washington, D.C.: OTA, June 1978).

4. Brian Johnson, "Who Cares?", *Mazingira*, no. 6, (June 1979).

5. Norman L. Brown and James W. Howe, "Solar Energy for Village Development," *Science* 199 (February 1978): 652.

6. Vaclav Smil, "Intermediate Technology in China," *Bulletin of Atomic Scientists* 33, no. 2 (1977): 27-28.

7. See Carroll L. Wilson, *Coal—Bridge to the Future, Report of the World Coal Study (WOCOL)* (Cambridge, Mass.: Ballinger Books, 1980).

8. See World Bank, *Coal Development Potential and Prospects in the Developing Countries* (Washington, D.C.: World Bank, 1979).

9. The authors are particularly indebted to Gregory Thomas for his counsel on the preparation of this section.

10. World Bank, *Rural Electrification Sector Paper* (Washington, D.C.: World Bank, 1975), p. 17.

11. Ibid, p. 18.

12. See Dr. B.G. Desai, "Solar Electrification and Rural Electrification—A Techno-Economic Review," in F. deWinter and M. Cox, eds., *Sun—Mankind's Future Source of Energy* (Pergamon Press, 1978), 1:211-13.

13. From the testimony of Norman L. Brown before the Subcommittee on Domestic and International Scientific Planning, Analysis and Cooperation of the Committee on Science and Technology, U.S. House of Representatives, July 26, 1978, pp. 9-10. (Mimeo.)

14. Anil Agarwal, *Whose Solar Power?*, Earthscan Press-Briefing Document No. 19 (London: Earthscan, 1979), p. 23.

15. Council on Environmental Quality, *Solar Energy—Progress and Promise* (CEQ, April 1978), p. IV.

16. President Carter's Message to the Congress on Solar Energy, June 20, 1979, (Office of White House Press Secretary), p. 4.

17. Robert Stobaugh and Daniel Yergin, "After the Second Shock: Pragmatic Energy Strategies," *Foreign Affairs* 57, no. 4 (Spring 1979): 857. Reprinted by permission from *Foreign Affairs* (Spring 1979); Copyright 1979 by Council on Foreign Relations, Inc.

18. See J.E.M. Arnold, "Wood Energy and Rural Communities," *Natural Resources Forum* 3, no. 3 (April 1979): 229-52.

19. A list of improved stove designs can be found in J. Goldemberg and

R.I. Brown, "Cooking Stoves: the State of the Art," University of São Paulo, São Paulo, Brazil, 1979. (Unpublished.)

20. See *Planting For the Future: Forestry for Human Needs*, by Erik Eckholm (Washington, D.C.: Worldwatch Paper 26, February 1979), pp. 48–56.

21. *Workshop on Solar Energy for the Villages of Tanzania* sponsored by Tanzania National Scientific Research Council and U.S. National Academy of Sciences, August 1977. Results of the Workshop are also contained in an article by Norman L. Brown and James W. Howe, "Solar Energy for Village Development" in *Science* (Vol. 199, 10 February 1978), pp. 651–657.

Chapter 3

Policies and Programs For Third World Energy Aid

During the past two years a great surge of activity—summit meetings of heads of state, international working groups, conferences, seminars, and task forces—has created the impression that Western governments are ablaze with interest in the challenge to development presented by the worldwide scarcity of energy. This may be true. But too much of this concern turns out, on close examination, to be frenetic communication among governments determined to appear active despite their uncertainty of how to proceed. Efforts such as the MacPhail Group (a special working group of the OECD set up to act upon the recommendations of the 1978 Bonn summit[a]) or the June 1979 meeting of donor agencies hosted by the World Bank in Paris have been criticized for contributing little more than a review of existing programs and a justification of current levels of effort.

Is such criticism really justified? Only if one ignores the domestic political pressures on donor governments faced with inflation *and* recession. But surely the new programs to help developing countries meet their energy needs ought to be seen in a politically wide perspective. We believe that new priorities emerging in the U.N. agencies, the multilateral development banks, the aid programs of the West and OPEC, and the highest level economic consultation of

[a]The MacPhail Group was officially designated the "Working Party of the Council to Develop a Coordinated Effort to Help Developing Countries Bring into Use Technologies Related to Renewable Energy." It came into being on November 27, 1978, and submitted its final report to the OECD Council on May 10, 1979.

Western and OPEC summits all point in one direction. For a variety of reasons, and often from conflicting motives, aid programs reflect a new open-mindedness and willingness to act on the Third World energy dilemma. This tendency is growing stronger daily. But these agencies and governments are proceeding with great caution, both because an immense effort is needed, and because nobody knows what types of programs are most likely to succeed.

This hesitation, bearing in mind the scale of need, makes it all too easy to criticize agencies that have just started on new initiatives for not having started sooner or yet gotten further. But it is quite unrealistic to do so if we consider that interest in alternative and renewable energy sources is generally very recent. Many starts are being made. The question is how well conceived and directed are they?

As a step toward answering this question, in this chapter the work of major international and bilateral institutions on new forms of energy assistance is reviewed: Traditional and established forms of energy aid are not discussed except to the extent that these shed light on problems with new initiatives.

Examining the changing role of international institutions in stimulating new energy initiatives and transferring new energy technology requires that several factors be considered. We must look at the political history of these institutions, relevant because bitter experiences of the past so often limit the choices for the future; we must examine the constitutional tasks of each organization and the extent to which these have been or can be stretched or redefined so as to add new sorts of activity; and we must look at the actual programs of these agencies and at the attitudes of their management and staff, their policy goals, and the practical constraints that they face. Then we must consider, insofar as is possible, the actual (or potential) value of these programs: Who is supposed to benefit, and who is likely to do so in practice?

Finally, in order to suggest realistic priorities as well as specific recommendations, it is useful to recall certain political and institutional developments of the last two years. One clear signpost is the institutional initiative that arose from the Bonn summit, referred to above. Second, the World Bank has established a large and ambitious new program to accelerate petroleum production in developing countries. Third, the United Nations General Assembly has scheduled a Conference on New and Renewable Sources of Energy, which will be held in 1981. Fourth, OPEC Governments have announced their intention to consider transferring the OPEC Fund into a new, fullfledged development program. These four omens, combined, have a formidable potential to affect the energy plight of many poorer countries. Whether this will happen remains to be seen. To set energy aid programs in their political context, we begin with the attention they recently received at the summit.

POLITICAL ACTION AT THE SUMMIT

At the Bonn Economic summit of July 1978, the communiqué of the leaders of government declared that:

> To help developing countries, we will intensify our national development assistance programs in the energy field and we will develop a coordinated effort to bring into use renewable energy technologies and to elaborate the details within one year. We stress the need for improvement and coordination of assistance for developing countries in the energy field.

In response to this request, the Council of the OECD established the MacPhail Group, whose mandate was not to make policy recommendations to governments but "to seek to develop a common approach on what actions should be taken in bilateral and multilateral programs." The MacPhail Group at first encountered difficulties in organizing its work. The absence of French membership in the International Energy Agency meant that the IEA could not officially back up the MacPhail Group. In addition, some countries that have provided substantial energy assistance to developing countries, such as the Netherlands, reacted with considerable diffidence to the initiative of a summit "club" of which they are not members.

Some participating governments suspected that alternative energy found its way into the communiqué of a Western economic summit as the result of an American and French desire to publicize renewable energy accomplishments to date. In fact, the issue emerged as a result of a combination of the pressures and the interests described in Chapter 1. Ideally, the MacPhail Group should have been able to seize its potential advantage over previous initiatives (such as the ill-fated proposals of 1976-77 for an International Energy Institute) and focus on the requirements for "a coordinated effort," to recall the language of the communiqué. In fact nothing approaching that result was politically feasible. The Americans have an active program but fail really to agree among themselves on its purpose and priorities. The French, also active, would balk at any proposal that emphasized multilateral aid at the expense of their bilateral program with former French colonies. The British and Canadians appear somewhat enthusiastic but so far have achieved little, and the West Germans appear concerned lest the promotion of their potential exports in the field of solar energy suffer at the hands of countries with former colonial connections.

This is not to say that the MacPhail Group was unable to achieve any significant advances; simply that its initial reach considerably exceeded its grasp. But the group did achieve two things. First, a process of consultation and coordination among donor governments has been initiated for the first time in the energy field. This ought to enable them to be more aware of one another's activities and so take better advantage of the lessons of experience, as well as to point to areas of potential collaboration between developed and developing countries. In fact, the need for simple exchange of project information is great: One donor government was planning a program of energy assessments in several developing countries in order to develop a national energy assessment methodology and was considering Peru as a country in which to work. That aid agency did not know that the U.S. Department of Energy had just completed its energy assessment in Peru.

The second contribution of the MacPhail Group was to reexamine and assimilate all of the different tasks that need to be accomplished in order to help developing countries meet their energy needs. This, too, was an important function because it carried out, in one place, a comparative evaluation of competing proposals and policy analyses. The report of the group argues that "the problem of an adequate dissemination of the information on renewables is probably the most important immediate hindrance." It suggests that there is a need to encourage the exchange between developed and developing countries, and among developing countries, of technological information, as well as a need to develop a widely available stored-data exchange system.[b]

The MacPhail Group's report and recommendations suffered from a weakness inherent in its mandate—namely, that the terms of reference limited research and recommendations to renewable-energy

[b]The other proposals of the group, while quite general, included the following:

1. "Greater emphasis" on renewable energy projects and the provision of "additional resources (financial and otherwise)" for them.
2. Assessment of renewable energy potential and resources for individual developing countries, including surveys to determine existing Third World research and development activities on renewable energy;
3. Research and development programs in OECD countries specifically aimed at meeting the needs of developing countries, and programs aimed at building up their production, installation, and maintenance capacity. The R&D recom-

problems and solutions in isolation from other sources of energy such as oil, gas, and nuclear power. But politically, a spearhead of action was needed. The MacPhail Group may have met that need by mobilizing interest in the problems and promise of renewable energy. Unfortunately, some of the recommendations suffer for this. For example, it does not seem terribly useful to carry out assessments of renewable energy resource "base needs" and "uses" in aid-receiving countries apart from the context of overall energy assessment and planning. How helpful is it to know how much firewood costs in Upper Volta, for example, if one is not also considering the price of kerosene and the interrelationship of the two? There is fortunately little question but that the staff of the OECD, the members of the MacPhail Group, and the relevant ministries and donor countries share the view that the MacPhail Group report must be seen as a pebble about which a ball of twine can be slowly wound.

A more serious problem with donor country coordination and planning exercises is the exclusion of developing country participation. On the one hand, it is self-evident that political planning among like-minded countries inevitably will exclude states that are not members of a particular "club", so the formal structure of the Mac-Phail Group was certainly avoidable. It might have been possible, however, to take the views of developing countries into account in formulating recommendations. Some countries, notably Sweden, tried to speak on behalf of the Third World, but that in itself seems unpromising. Despite recent rhetoric, aid activity in the sector of energy is still more donor-determined than in almost any of the others. This is partly due to its capital-intensive nature up to now. But it also reflects the highly sensitive political questions that inevitably arise in any discussion of energy policy.

In the aftermath of that first effort, preoccupation with their own energy problems sidetracked donor country concern for energy aid to the Third World. The Tokyo summit of June 1979 (to which the MacPhail Report was submitted) paid almost no attention to Third World energy problems, and the Venice Summit Communique in 1980 said nothing new, but offered vague support for World Bank

---

mendation also includes reference to technological adaptation, field testing and demonstration projects, and joint research and development activities.

4. Institution building, with particular reference to developing and improving energy planning capacity, and to assisting technical training programs to select, manage, and further develop renewable energy technologies; and

5. Encouragement of new approaches to project evaluation, including innovative methods of cost projection and social and environmental analysis; also, in connection with project formulation, avoiding unnecessary duplication of projects in the renewable energy field.

programs. By June 1979, of course, the Iranian revolution had put oil and OPEC not just on the front burner, but on every burner. The heads of governments agreed only to say that "we will do more to help developing countries increase the "use of renewable energy," and to support expansion of the World Bank's fossil fuels program.[c]

ENERGY AID PROGRAMS OF OECD MEMBER COUNTRIES

The International Energy Agency (IEA) and the Third World

Within the OECD, the principal organ of energy policy and analysis is the International Energy Agency, founded in 1974 as the Northern industrial powers' answer to OPEC. The IEA has only very lately started to interest itself in Third World problems. Its principal task was, and remains, the preparation of contingency plans involving oil allocation and demand-restraint measures to meet possible interruptions in oil supply. However, the intervening years have seen the agency establish an energy research and development program that is looking at long-term energy possibilities. This is an attempt to coordinate cooperative work among governments on coal technology, solar energy, production of hydrogen from water, utilization of waste heat and other forms of energy conservation, and various aspects of nuclear power. Is the IEA perhaps the logical coordinating point for Northern activity intended to help developing countries meet their energy needs?

Certainly the staff of the IEA is highly competent. And because of the importance of its subject matter, the IEA relates to its participating governments at a high level. This creates political flexibility as well as the capacity to respond quickly to changing circumstances. For example, in December 1978 the agency sponsored a workshop

[c]One initiative revealed at Tokyo may eventually prove to be an important link in a strategy of North-South energy cooperation, even though it was not proposed with the developing countries first in mind. This was the commitment to create an International Energy Technology Group:

New technologies in the field of energy are the key to the world's longer term freedom from fuel crises. Large public and private resources will be required for the development and commercial application of those technologies. We will ensure that these resources are made available. An *International Energy Technology Group* linked to the OECD, IEA and other appropriate international organizations will be created to review the actions being taken or planned domestically by each of our countries, and to report on the need and potential for international collaboration, including financing.

on Energy Demand in Developing Countries, which brought together developing country energy planners in Paris to discuss data-gathering methodology and designed a computer model for collection of available data in the future. This technical initiative was a useful political breakthrough that should not be underestimated. For the first time, the IEA's technical expertise (in this case, the gathering of analytical data) has been used to catalyze and advise the efforts of about twenty developing countries. The IEA plans to expand this effort, and in the words of one official, "to talk to anyone who will talk to us."

However, for two reasons unconnected with the agency's internal competence, the IEA seems to be unable to provide international leadership on energy aid. First, France is not a member of the IEA, preferring to negotiate with OPEC on a bilateral basis. This creates internal problems for the OECD (of which France is a member), but it also would tend to exclude from the IEA's purview the very active, growing French program in renewable energy. Second, the United States seems determined not to allow the North-South energy dialogue to shift from what it regards as the central question: the price and supply of oil. It would therefore tend to disfavor any initiative that diluted the IEA's original purpose, despite the large advantages of discarding the IEA's justifiable image of being the club of the major oil consumers.

The European Community

Apart from the participation of OECD countries in the World Bank and the regional development banks, the major multilateral energy effort belongs to the European Economic Community (EEC, traditionally known as the "Common Market"), and involves nine of its twenty-four member countries. The EEC, headquartered in Brussels, has four divisions concerned with energy questions: the Directorate-General for Energy, the Directorate-General for International Relations, the Directorate-General for Science and Technology, and the Directorate-General for Development Cooperation (the European Development Fund—EDF). Each will have some influence on the shape of Community policy toward Third World energy assistance. The complex political arrangements of the European Community are beyond the scope of this book, but their influence sets EEC energy aid in context. Energy is one of the issues where most members of the Community, with the exception of the producers of North Sea oil, regard their mutual interests as being very closely aligned. In the energy field, more than in many others, the Community is making progress in developing a common foreign (or "external") policy. This could have far-reaching results for energy assistance programs, which are principally the concern of the EDF.

There does not as yet seem to be a coherent Community energy program, even though the need is felt for an agreed approach. The Energy Directorate has recently sponsored a Low Energy (Strategy) Working Group, which has achieved notable publicity in Europe but which still contends with a strong orientation toward nuclear power within the Community. The Energy Directorate has been advocating a solar energy demonstration program to be carried out in Europe and had originally hoped for substantial funding, which has been de-layed and limited by the British. But perhaps the plight of the Com-munity's energy planners was best illustrated by its sponsorship of an international Conference on Solar Energy for Development held in Varese, Italy, in March 1979.[1] Most officials in Brussels agree that this conference was important—a major Community initiative—but few give the same reasons. Several of the organizers said it had been conceived as the Community's contribution to preparations for the United Nations Conference on Science and Technology for Develop-ment. Others described the conference as the EEC effort to design an "energy plan of action for the negotiation of the successor agree-ment to the Lomé Convention," and said that specific guidelines and targets were the goal. (The Lomé Convention, 1975–1980, was the agreement between the Community and fifty-three African, Carib-bean, and Pacific states that defined terms and levels of development assistance for that five-year period.) Still others saw the Varese Conference as a general contribution to the political processes of North-South dialogue. Many developing country researchers and policymakers who were present in Varese considered it a "trade show" for European solar technology. In part, this confusion results from the hybrid nature of EEC activity.

It is useful to think of the development aid activity of the EEC as being more in the nature of bilateral, rather than multilateral, aid. The Community accepts that some of its members compete with one another for Third World markets, but it is nevertheless com-mitted to direct and immediate transfers that heavily emphasize exported technology. It might, in these circumstances, be useful for the Community to reconsider its role as an honest broker between the exporters and the recipient developing countries.

The program of the EDF is the result of a unique process of nego-tiation between the European Community and the fifty-three as-sisted Atlantic, Caribbean, and Pacific (ACP) states. The first product was the Lomé Convention of 1975, and Lomé II has just taken effect this year, devoting considerable attention to energy aid. The Lomé negotiations are watched very carefully by donor and aid-receiving nations alike; not so much because these negotiations go a long way toward transforming "aid" into genuine "cooperation"—which they do to a more than purely cosmetic degree—but because the first Lomé agreement was generally admired for its innovative qualities (especially its stabilization fund for commodity prices).

The EDF seems ready for a significant expansion in the renewable energy field. Late in 1978 its field officers conducted a detailed survey on the availability of reliable energy data and the adequacy of energy planning and policy instruments in the ACP states. On the basis of this information, the EDF proposed a detailed program of action to the ACP states to include: energy inventories (including "adequate attention" to noncommercial energy); renewable energy projects to include wind, solar, geothermal, and small-scale hydro; a new rural energy program; and the establishment of means—mainly the provision or strengthening of appropriate institutions—for the ACP states to increase their "management and control" of their energy resources. Lomé II, as finally agreed, provides wide scope for these programs and also calls for significantly increased assistance to develop fossil fuel resources, principally oil.

The sticking point in this program may be the terms of financing: Because the EDF has a fixed sum available for disbursement over five years, the strategy of the ACP states is generally to try to identify other funding programs within the European Community that might provide supplemental funds. In other words, if a research project were planned for a particular developing country, the ACP states might suggest that the EEC's Directorate for Science and Technology should bear the costs, leaving EDF funds untouched and therefore available for other projects. This type of negotiation points to a critical trend in the thinking of development financers: Following the pattern of the Dutch aid program in Indonesia, the view is rapidly being accepted that the side (donor or recipient) promoting a project or program should bear the lion's share of the costs. Under this approach, if a donor is particularly interested in a project, it should provide most of the funds. If the host country is the principal advocate of an undertaking, its counterpart contribution should increase. This arrangement recognizes the reality of development finance, avoiding the traditional lip service to the notion that all projects are initiated by host governments.

Bilateral Energy Aid

Direct foreign assistance from bilateral aid agencies and the EDF accounted for about 73 percent of Official Development Assistance in 1977[2] ($10.8 billion of a total ODA of $14.7 billion). During the past five years, meanwhile, approximately $130 million has been spent on renewable energy projects. Although these agencies have paid increasing attention to firewood, solar, and other renewable energy projects, they have not as yet given much thought to aid in the petroleum or natural gas sectors and have provided little support to strengthen the Third World's own energy institutions. Development aid per se, however, constitutes only one part of overall bilateral energy assistance. Energy ministries sometimes carry out direct assistance programs (for example, the U.S. Department of Energy's "assessments" in Egypt and Peru) or undertake joint-venture activities of research and development (for example, the German Ministry of Research and Technology's programs in India and Egypt). All of these programs share certain tendencies that distinguish them from the programs of multilateral organizations (discussed later in this chapter).

The main distinguishing feature of bilateral aid, inevitably, is its close link to foreign policy objectives of donor countries. This has always been particularly evident with French aid: Energy assistance to countries that are not ex-colonies of France is administered directly from the Foreign Ministry, while the Ministry of Cooperation pays exclusive attention to former French colonies. To preserve close economic ties, former colonies are given special consideration not just by the French but also by the British and the Dutch. More recently, President Carter's efforts to limit the spread of nuclear weapons have linked energy assistance explicitly to American foreign policy objectives, although the U.S. Agency for International Development (AID) stresses its concern with the humanitarian objective of assisting "the poorest of the poor," rather than this connection.

A second characteristic of bilateral aid programs is their ability to provide assistance on highly concessional terms. Development banks generally lend money, whereas national aid agencies combine grants and loans on negotiated terms. In practice, this often means that bilateral projects are less subject to strict economic and financial criteria, so that, under such programs, innovative or high-risk activities often may stand a better chance of support. However, this leeway sometimes has an unfortunate side-effect. Some bilateral agencies seek diverse sets of circumstances, for example to test a new technology, but pay insufficient attention to the economic viability of the venture. The result can be "successful" tests that ignore the economic circumstances of the intended beneficiaries.

The third consideration to note is the obligation of most aid programs to promote national exports in the projects they fund. Only

U.S. AID is not required to promote American products, but this largely reflects the preference of large U.S. businesses to work without "government interference" abroad. AID does give overwhelming preference to American contracts and contractors when it provides services in a developing country.

These factors affect the types of energy aid activities supported by some OECD governments. Traditionally their programs have supported electric power generation, through construction of both thermal and hydropower facilities, and more recently have been committing about 10 percent of their energy funds to rural electrification projects. Large programs such as these could hardly be changed overnight: U.S. AID, for example, says it has deemphasized rural electrification, but in 1979 had $82 million in such projects at various stages of development (twice as much money as it then devoted to renewable energy projects).

Now momentum is gathering in favor of renewable energy projects. The more recent renewable energy activities of seven bilateral aid agencies (Canada, France, Germany, Kuwait, Netherlands, the United Kingdom, and the United States) are summarized in Table 4, Appendix 4. But there is no clear agreement on preferred methods. Rather than scrutinize a broad range of programs, in this section we describe some promising initiatives and special problems that are being encountered.

French Aid for Renewable Energy

The French aid program in renewable energy is better established, and until 1979 was better funded, than any other bilateral or multilateral program. Sixty-five million francs ($15.5 million) were spent between 1976 and 1978 in Africa alone, and the corresponding figure for 1979 was budgeted at 29 million francs. Despite their clear lead in the solar field (at least if measured by the number of projects operational), the French have become acutely aware of a growing American effort and are worried that the French solar industry's export markets in developing countries could be overwhelmed by heavily financed U.S. programs.

Even before 1975, the French government sponsored an active solar research program. In that year, the Délégué aux Energies Nouvelles was established within the Ministry of Industry. At roughly the same time, the drought crisis in the Sahel prompted talks with Senegal, Mali, and Upper Volta, which led the Ministry of Cooperation (or FAC, for the Fonds d'Assistance et de Coordination) to set up a special program to utilize renewable energy sources in Africa. More recently, all solar-related renewable energy research and development in France has been brought under a new agency, the Commissariat à l'Énergie Solaire (COMES), which also seeks out international cooperative ventures for the French solar industry. (In 1979, all renewable energy aid projects from the Ministry of Co-operation were transferred to COMES.) The well organized links between French aid and the solar industry were completed with the acquisition by the national Atomic Energy Commission (CEA) of a controlling interest in one of the world's best known solar energy firms, Sofretes. (This acquisition is explained by a cabinet decision to diversify the commission's activities rather than underutilize the government's vast nuclear research structure. However, there are also indications within Sofretes of an increasing interest in relatively large-scale solar installations).

The program for renewable energy of the Ministry of Cooperation has three distinct components: applied technological studies, geographical studies to ascertain the characteristics and needs of regions and countries, and operational projects. French aid has taken an interest in biomass, solar cookers and refrigeration, and wind energy. But its most publicized effort has been the installation of over 100 solar irrigation pumps in the Sahel and Mexico. As mentioned in Chapter 2, projects using thermal solar collectors have experienced severe maintenance problems. Many of these are out of service at the present time, and recently French companies have contemplated switching to photovoltaic systems.

In response to its early setbacks—attributable to a premature commitment to a technology designed and tested under French conditions—FAC has taken certain remedial measures. Its previously hesitant attitude toward joint projects has changed visibly, so that not only is the ministry eager to work with EDF, but it has even co-sponsored a project with U.S. AID in Bakel, Upper Volta. A second step has been a new policy on counterpart funding. Before 1978, all renewable energy projects were 100 percent "subvention" (grant aid), but recently host countries have been asked to make at least a small contribution, establishing their stake in making projects work under diverse local conditions. Finally, French officials have become convinced that extensive applied research and adaptation have to precede wide distribution of solar technology. They argue, therefore, that the greatest barrier to solar energy's having a major impact in the Third World is the lack of start-up finance to cover these early—albeit very large—additional costs.

Despite French aid's usual caution, the French government took risks before any other government or international institution was prepared to do so, in order to transfer its domestic solar products to developing countries. But some of the ill-conceived thermal collector projects caused many observers to question whether development objectives had not been totally subordinated to industrial promotion. There is little doubt that FAC's experience working with local institutions in the West African countries (where so much renewable energy aid has been concentrated) could help to rectify past mistakes, *if* this experience were seriously applied to the problems of adaptation and localized application. Were this to be done, one might expect the French solar energy aid program to maintain its lead position for the foreseeable future.

The U.S. Approach

Unlike French officials, American policymakers are still searching for an agreed approach toward renewable energy aid. Two quite different perceptions of the purposes of energy aid can be found in official U.S. thinking, and even within one agency (AID) two different approaches are advocated. AID's energy assistance program is required to follow the congressionally mandated "new directions" of foreign aid, which after 1974 directed agency attention exclusively toward programs to meet basic human needs. This legislative influence on the details of foreign aid is peculiar to the American system of government. It has resulted in detailed legislation, which directs that energy sources and conservation methods utilized in AID projects should be "suitable" to developing countries, and that technologies used are to meet many criteria, such as "appropriate," "decentralized," "renewable," and so on.[d]

In response to congressional direction, but also to its own changing perception of Third World energy needs, AID has established an Office of Energy which has overall planning responsibility for AID energy programs and guides field missions on the types of help that

[d]Section 103(c) authorizes assistance for the rural poor through expansion of local or small-scale rural energy infrastructure.

Section 106(2) authorizes assistance for suitable energy sources and conservation methods, collection and analysis of information concerning energy supplies and needs, and pilot projects to test new methods of production or conservation of energy.

Section 107 authorizes activities in the field of intermediate technology, . . . to promote the development and dissemination of "appropriate" technologies.

Section 119 authorizes assistance in research, development, and use of small-scale, decentralized renewable energy sources for rural areas. Programs shall be directed toward the earliest practicable development and use of energy technologies that (1) are environmentally acceptable; (2) require minimum capital investment; (3) are most acceptable to, and affordable by, the people using them; (4) are simple and inexpensive to use and maintain; and (5) are transferable from one region of the world to another.

AID headquarters is willing to offer. Its staff at first was principally concerned with testing and applying new and renewable energy technologies, but recently has gotten underway a number of small energy assessment, data collection, and technology-adaptation projects. Growing sums of money have been, or will be, made available to AID's Energy Office. In AID as a whole (most money is budgeted through the regional divisions), over 42 million in U.S. dollars was allocated to renewable energy programs for FY 1980. (See Table 4N.2, Appendix 4).

AID's new energy office has been criticized in the United States for being excessively technology-oriented. However, most project decisions in AID are made by one of four regional bureaus, which have considerable initiative. One of these—the Africa Bureau—has made the firewood shortage its highest priority. Although four or five small solar projects have been carried out, this bureau is now concentrating on reforestation programs and fuelwood conservation. It proposes to finance village woodlots on a wide scale (and now has specific congressional authority to do so), on the theory that the population it seeks to reach cannot afford any of the new forms of expensive renewable energy.[e]

Considerable disagreement emerges from within AID's ranks as to whether firewood (which supplements existing energy sources) or new technologies (which replace current energy sources) should receive his/her budgetary priority. But it must be recalled that AID's target populations are the poorest people in the poorest countries, so that AID does not promote the very broad range of energy solutions called for by diverse Third World conditions. And finally, some support has gathered in the Congress and in AID's new parent organization, the International Development Cooperation Agency (IDCA), behind a new energy program area for AID—to finance the discovery and production of oil, natural gas, and coal resources. A large program seems unlikely, however, since the Carter administration has argued for larger World Bank appropriations on the ground that *it* was the development institution best suited to undertake a fossil fuels program.

In sum, AID's energy work is confusingly narrow, since projects targeted in isolation at the poorest people (who probably cannot pay for energy they consume) place the energy needs of modern

[e]Sections 101(b) and 104(a) of the International Development Cooperation Act of 1979 PL. 96-53, 1979, provides that "the President is authorized to provide assistance for foresting projects, emphasizing community woodlots, agro-forestry, reforestation, protection of watershed forests, and more effective forest management."

growth, as well as the needs of middle-income countries, beyond the ambit of AID assistance. The potential for energy conservation is great in the modern sector of most Third World countries, yet AID will find it difficult to act in the middle-income countries that stand to gain most by conserving energy. Likewise, a narrow focus on the needs of the rural poor confines energy planning and assessment assistance to a misleadingly narrow slice of overall energy use. We believe that it is important for AID to continue to provide "basic human needs" for energy. But the full range of developing country *and* U.S. goals in coping with the energy needs of the Third World is not sufficiently encompassed within the scope of basic human needs.

The other important U.S. program, administered by the Department of Energy, began its life in September 1977 as the LDC Energy Program (since renamed the International Energy Development Program). Its purpose was to encourage the use of non-nuclear energy alternatives, by sending technical energy-planning teams to selected countries. The job of these teams—so far assessments have been completed in Egypt and Peru, and six more are planned—is to advise the host country on its economic alternatives among possible energy strategies. This program could be absorbed by Title V of the U.S. Nuclear Non-Proliferation Act of 1978, which requires the U.S. government to endeavor to establish "programs to assist in the development of non-nuclear energy resources," although for a variety of reasons President Carter has not yet authorized a federal agency to carry but this particular mandate of the act.[f]

Only the lack of effective oil conservation measures has aroused more negative reaction in the Third World than Carter's nonproliferation efforts, despite the fact that no more than ten or twelve developing countries can realistically expect to be using nuclear power by 1990. It is not just the thought that Third World governments might be internationally "irresponsible" that most offends them, whether or not nuclear power is a realistic option. They regard Carter's initiatives as a violation of the fundamental bargain underpinning the nuclear non-proliferation treaty (safeguards in exchange for assured fuel supplies), and an infringement on their national sovereignty.

The paradox of the present American program may be that the best way to deter a premature commitment to nuclear power is to

---

[f]Title V of the Nuclear Non-Proliferation Act also authorizes a program of *training* for Third World energy officials and planners. This, too, has not yet been implemented.

provide national energy planning assistance that is *not* overtly anti-nuclear. Seven members of the Foreign Relations Committee of the U.S. Senate, recognizing this problem, advocated that "nuclear power should not be excluded from the areas of energy-assessment and -planning activities."[3] In almost every case, the economic arguments speak for themselves. In Egypt, for example, the assessment showed that over two-thirds of Egypt's gross national product would be needed to achieve its twenty-year plan for nuclear electricity generation. The plan has subsequently been quietly dropped.

This particular American program has been burdened not just by its suspected lack of objectivity (a suspicion that was certainly undercut, at least partially, in Egypt and Peru), but also by the more general Third World hostility toward the Non-Proliferation Act. However, the saving grace of these energy assessments may be simply that they are so obviously needed. Egyptian officials said that the joint U.S.-Egyptian exercise was the first occasion on which the horizon of national energy planning had reached beyond the life of a particular project. The Egyptians cooperated with the program (and agreed to public release of the report and recommendations) despite the fact that the assessments demonstrated that Egypt's ambitious nuclear plans could not be justified as the best response to prospective energy demand. The sophistication and toughness with which Third World officials protect their national interests should itself not be underestimated—if political chaff is suspected in these assessments, it can and will be discarded. It is ironic, however, that the first extensive program of national energy planning aid should have to be encumbered with these problems.

Another dispute of large significance has arisen over the U.S. energy assessment program. The Department of Energy has used a relatively comprehensive econometric approach, which accepts the host country's development plans and then suggests four or five different combinations of technologies to supply projected levels of energy demand. The possible availability of different energy resources and technologies is varied in order to lay out alternative energy strategies. This work has been done by large teams of American experts who visit the host country for relatively short periods.

Critics, including U.S. AID, argue that the first step should be to consider a range of economic development options, then to project energy requirements and strategies for each. In this way, a government can base its energy strategy on development goals, rather than the other way around, or can at least factor energy restraints into its development strategy to the same extent that it considers developmental constraints in its energy planning. This rather simplified dichotomy obscures a hidden political catch: Most governments of poor countries jealously protect their sovereign acts of national development planning, but in reality accept considerable outside planning help. Hence Egypt's relief at the reappraisal of a national nuclear strategy that had called for twelve nuclear power stations by the year 1990. Energy planning assistance that does not examine development options may seem, superficially at least, to be politically preferable. But this approach seems unlikely to provide the help that is most badly needed. The answer may be the gradual removal of this trap by helping Third World governments to develop the capability to do their own energy assessments, and by providing training and methodologies for energy policy planning.

Dutch Aid: A Political Breakthrough?

Although the Dutch Directorate General for International Cooperation (DGIC) has limited project experience compared to U.S. AID or the French, its abstract concern with renewable energy sources dates from the 1977 "Report on the Difficulties Involved in Applying Solar Energy in Developing Countries" prepared by the Dutch Ministry of Foreign Affairs. Since that time enthusiasm has grown at such a rate that in November, 1979 the Dutch became the first agency to announce a radical redirection for energy lending to the renewables (U.S. AID policy has evolved in fits and starts, largely due to Congressional and agency interaction, whereas the new Dutch policy has been announced in one major shift). At the same time, the Dutch Foreign Ministry called for a boost of the development cooperation budget to 1½ percent of net national income annually.

The stated aim of the new Dutch energy strategy is to help improve the situation of oil-importing developing countries. According to the November 1979 statement of the Ministry of Foreign Affairs, this requires a range of actions that reach beyond aid per se:

> External energy policy must . . . be based on awareness of the fact that measures designed to secure domestic energy supplies must pay due regard to the shared responsibility for guaranteeing the supplies of the international community. National goals must not be inconsistent with international ones. It is important that the industrialized countries do not regulate future energy supplies on a unilateral basis, but are prepared to hold negotiations with oil-producing countries and other developing countries in the context of the whole range of factors constituting North-South relations. A reduction in the demand for energy, particularly, in industrialized countries, must be encouraged in order to ensure consistency between domestic and international aims. At the same time research into energy conservation methods and alternative sources of energy for developing countries should be intensified.[4]

The Dutch have promised to expand their renewable aid for developing countries by three principal measures. First the Dutch will increase the funding of their renewable program. They will provide over $13 million in the next three years for financing research into the application of renewable sources of energy for developing countries. Also included is a pledge of over $50 million annually to afforestation programs and dissemination of more efficient means of wood use, especially in the Sahelian region of Africa. A final financial measure will consist of a substantial contribution (some $10 million) to a multilateral fund, new or existing, for exploring for and exploiting sources of energy in developing countries (the Dutch government also pledged to promote by diplomatic initiative the establishment of such a fund).

Second, the Netherlands will continue to augment its training programs, particularly by increasing emphasis on the energy planning capacities of aid-receiving countries. The third and final measure is a pledge to expand the Dutch activities in informational exchanges, both at a technical level and at the international level. In this regard, the Netherlands has promised support for expanded World Bank, DAC, and EEC activities in exchanging information in the energy field.

The new Dutch policy has a ring of coherence to it, which seems lacking elsewhere, including the United States. This may reflect the process by which it was developed. Several Dutch aid officials, expert in renewable energy resources and technology, began to circulate a draft policy paper late in 1978. Because of its budgetary implications a new policy could not be implemented without Cabinet approval, and so it received careful scrutiny (and was the subject of intense debate) within the aid ministry. By the time it emerged it reflected a concentration on Dutch strengths, rather than a scatter-shot attempt to do everything at once.

Shifting Focus in Other
Bilateral Aid Programs

Bilateral aid programs of other OECD countries have not yet followed the French and American lead in funding renewable energy projects, nor have they followed the Dutch in announcing an overall policy. The British Overseas Development Administration (U.K. ODA) has shown considerable interest in alternative energy programs, which it sees as an integral part of its new interest in appropriate technology. So far, the U.K. ODA has commissioned studies but has moved cautiously toward funding projects.

The West German Bundestag, perhaps feeling a leadership obligation after playing host to the 1978 summit, has pledged (but not appropriated) a total of 150 million marks ($81 million) to an alternative energy aid program. The West German aid agency (the BMZ) prefers to finance energy projects in relatively advanced developing countries whose planning capability already exists. In the alternative energy field, however, almost no developing country has an adequate infrastructure to cope with the problems, and the projects are difficult to implement for social and other reasons. It seems likely, therefore, that traditional German foreign aid methods are not readily adaptable to a renewable energy program, unless an increased commitment to planning and institutional support functions is made.

Apart from these specific programs and financial allocations, a number of aid-giving governments have recently recognized the inadequacy of traditional aid institutions for promoting technological innovation and adaptation. Canada's International Development Research Centre and the United States' Appropriate Technology International each has been considering how to help developing countries with renewable energy programs. The German BMZ has set up a new division to carry out technical assistance programs, German Appropriate Technology Exchange, whose planning emphasizes energy projects among its priorities. All of these initiatives have one thing in common. They spring from the realization that technical and expert assistance is at least as important to the introduction of renewable energy programs in developing countries as the traditional development aid processes of project identification and financing. It is increasingly clear, from successes as well as failures, that alternative energy technology is not easily transferred by large-scale, repetitive projects. In response, rethinking and adaptation of programs is underway within many bilateral aid programs.

OPEC AID FOR ENERGY

The growing aid programs of some OPEC countries have always allocated a large percentage of their funds to energy projects, and almost all of these have followed in the pattern of loans, made by the World Bank and others, for large electric power generation and distribution projects. These energy projects face constraints shared by all OPEC aid agencies: Because OPEC countries themselves are underdeveloped technically, and short of trained professionals, small agency staffs disburse large sums of money. As a result a great deal of cofinancing is carried out in order to compensate for the lack of manpower to prepare projects. The effect of this situation is quite clear: Large or innovative technical redirections in the aid programs of OPEC members are only likely to happen in concert with the redirected efforts of other aid donors.

Despite these problems, the Kuwait Fund and the OPEC Fund have both shown interest in making loans for renewable energy projects as well as considerable enthusiasm for experimenting with other institutions. The OPEC Fund specially allocated $1.5 million to a project of the United Nations Development Programme for a comprehensive energy assessment and planning project in Central America. This was, in fact, the first venture by an OPEC aid program away from electric power projects in the energy field. More recently, the OPEC Fund approved an allocation of $5 million to the Latin American Energy Organization (OLADE), for a variety of technical assistance projects in the field of renewable energy. These two projects are indicative of an approach increasingly favored by OPEC countries to stretch the effective influence of their substantial development assistance allocations. In the view of a U.N. study, trust funds, particularly for energy, may hold special appeal for OPEC donors:

". . . trust funds placed by . . . OPEC donors with other major multilateral financial institutions might well encourage the latter to reconsider sympathetically the launching of expansion of schemes and initiatives proposed by developing countries but so far rejected on the grounds of their alleged nonviability. Although initially such schemes might be financed exclusively from the trust fund, their subsequent viability would undoubtedly help to overcome reservations that have impeded the launching of these schemes with the institutions' own funds. In this way, trust funds established by OPEC countries with existing institutions could act as powerful catalysts for the mobilization of international resources in a manner consistent with the needs of developing countries as they themselves see them."[5]

ENERGY ASSISTANCE FROM INTERNATIONAL ORGANIZATIONS

The World Bank, the major regional development banks, the United Nations Development Programme, and the U.N. system of agencies have provided substantial energy assistance to less developed countries—over $9.9 billion for the period 1973-1978. (See Table 4, Appendix 4 for details.) These concessional programs have a reach that far exceeds the obviously large direct effects of such vast sums, both because they stimulate—and sometimes guarantee—private investment, and because the conception and implementation of these projects influences, both intellectually and pragmatically, many other projects carried out by national governments.

Neither the Inter-American Development Bank (IDB) nor the Asian Development Bank (ADB) has so far shown much inclination to shift the allocation of their energy aid resources away from large-scale electric power projects. Both of these banks are acutely sensitive to the rapidly changing character of their borrowers' energy needs, however, and are looking for opportunities to expand their energy portfolios. By the end of 1979, the ADB had lent nearly $50 million for coal projects, while the IDB is eager to promote additional capital flows into Latin American energy production. The IDB has proposed to its members that they set up an Inter-American Energy and Minerals Guarantee Fund, to insure both equity and debt financing against political, and certain carefully defined commercial, risks.

The World Bank has gone furthest in setting up a fossil fuels program (discussed later in this chapter), which promotes exploration for, and production of, petroleum. But none of these banks has yet adopted an overall policy for renewable energy projects. It now seems only a matter of time before this happens, at least in the World Bank, which has already organized itself to prepare a program. In the area of alternative and renewable energy programs, particularly for use in rural areas, the World Bank's approach may diverge from that taken by bilateral aid programs. Rather than simply prepare to fund capital-intensive alternative energy systems, which in practice means almost exclusively solar energy projects, the bank is also trying to devise a program based on:

> . . . maintaining or even increasing the exploitation of the energy sources in rural areas, with considerable economic, social, and environmental advantages. This would not require sophisticated new technological developments, but an application or adaptation of basic expertise that exists in the developing countries.[6]

This approach was conceived in 1978 and seemed politically acceptable to an international institution that does not face direct pressure to stimulate growth of embryonic energy technology industries. But in today's volatile circumstances, it may also prove too narrow a base for an expanded World Bank effort. To obtain fast, wide-reaching results, one approach being considered is to utilize the technical capabilities of various sectoral departments (for example, forestry, water, and so forth) to identify and design new types of energy projects. This seems sound, particularly because it emphasizes the need not just to carry out energy projects per se, but also to analyze and meet the energy needs of all types of development projects.

The first example of this approach has been the World Bank's effort to enlarge and improve its forestry lending program. Although its critics charge that the program still principally underwrites industrial forestry, bank officials point out that they are now allocating resources to reforestation and tree-planting programs to provide fuelwood supplies. These loans generally approach a size of $50 million or more, so it is possible to divert some funds—usually 1 or 2 percent of the loan—to energy-related research and development. Plans call for most new forestry projects to allocate funds for improving stove design, training stove builders who can set up village stove-building businesses, and eventually offering credit support to help them get started in business.

But beyond such efforts added onto existing programs, under present circumstances the World Bank and the other international development financing institutions must overcome significant difficulties if they are going to devote meaningful levels of funding to renewable energy projects in the near, or even foreseeable, future. In general, research and experimental projects are too small to be considered for loans by the major development banks. To appraise and finance more than a few of these would consume a disproportionate amount of staff effort. Second, the demand for foreign exchange is so great in almost every developing country that these institutions always approach with great caution any innovations that might lead them away from providing foreign exchange for essential external equipment.

Finally, the development banks do not believe their greatest expertise falls in the technical assistance field; they are not comfortable with the institution-building and training projects that should accompany any new lending program for alternative energy projects.

The view has long been held in some international development-financing institutions—although there is widespread disagreement on this issue—that a long-run transformation away from an oil-based economy will depend, for most developing countries, on development *in the industrialized countries* of new energy technologies that are successfully transferable. This view is based on the premise that developing countries simply cannot afford the financial risks of innovation, but will commit their resources to new energy strategies only in the wake of parallel commitments made by the industrialized nations. This perception of less developed country needs has its foundations in the belief that transition away from fossil fuel dependence in the developing countries will only happen in the wake of a shift by industrialized countries. Even if this had been arguable in 1978, events since the Iranian revolution have made continued oil dependency unacceptably expensive for any Third World country that can find an alternative.

The official position taken by the World Bank of encouraging local, particularly rural, innovation and application seems at first glance to be contradicted by an approach that emphasizes eventual North-South transfers. In fact, an implicit motive of the World Bank's program may be to balance the inevitably export-oriented activities of most bilateral aid programs. Likewise, since it is improbable that new technologies that are commercially feasible in industrialized nations will be generally applicable in the impoverished rural areas of the Third World (on grounds of cost alone if nothing else), their transfer would only contribute to the alleviation of rural poverty if they were adapted and applied to local circumstances, probably by the aid recipients themselves.

An interesting choice looms before the industrialized countries in their dual position as direct providers of energy aid and also as the major contributors to institutions like the World Bank, the Inter-American Development Bank, and other regional funds. They can design their own bilateral programs and simultaneously encourage the major international organizations to cooperate in planning better-integrated energy programs for the Third World. But if in doing so they hope to hasten the commercial feasibility of new energy technologies, they will have to allow some relaxation of the strict financial rate-of-return criteria that they themselves have always favored in relation to energy projects. This sort of shift would take its place within the overall trends of development lending policy, toward favoring direct aid to the poorest, which many of these donor governments have been pressing on the major international development banks.

Under present circumstances the development banks have to await the commercial development of new energy technologies before including them in projects on a wide scale because their lending criteria, unlike the criteria of most bilateral aid programs, cannot accommodate large commitments to experimental, relatively risky projects that offer unfavorable immediate return. Multilateral efforts to utilize innovative energy technology products of developed country exporters would undoubtedly be viewed with less suspicion than bilateral aid programs designed to accomplish the same results. Therefore a critical breakthrough could be achieved by finding ways of enabling the multilateral banks, particularly the World Bank, to hasten the advent of *commercially feasible* renewable energy projects. An important job for bilateral agencies could be innovative "project identification" work, to show the development banks that there are enough "lendable" projects to justify their entry into the field. For example, since the World Bank is geared toward providing large loans for large-scale projects, it is more likely to be interested in sponsoring investment in a plant to manufacture solar equipment than for the purchase of small-scale finished systems. Locating and presenting these opportunities could be a priority function for governmental aid programs, as a way of involving multilateral and bilateral agencies more quickly. The export-oriented energy industries should also be encouraged, and helped, to work directly with the multilateral development aid agencies. Even if a small measure of immediate political control is surrendered by expediting multilateral entry into the renewable energy field, in the longer run, international cooperation on energy and development can be fostered by the fullest possible use of intermediaries trusted by the developing countries.

The World Bank's New Petroleum Program

The second major change occurring in these international development funding institutions required no such fundamental rethinking of roles and constitutional constraints. As originally conceived the World Bank's new Program to Accelerate Petroleum Production in the Developing Countries would have provided $13 billion in loans during the five-year period 1981–1985. However, even this vast initiative quickly seemed inadequate so that the World Bank has chosen to explore the establishment of a new lending facility, specifically for energy projects. Its objective would be to underwrite roughly $25 billion in energy loans by 1985.[7] About 60 percent of this lending will be devoted to production facilities for oil and gas projects, and the balance will be devoted to exploration and other preliminary petroleum operations. From the point of view of the World Bank and other international development banks, an attractive feature of oil and gas projects is that they are highly capital-intensive, thus allowing them to finance the type of project they were designed to carry out.

The World Bank's new program on either the committed or contemplated scale, is an important innovation. It represents, obviously, the first occasion on which a development agency has moved significantly beyond the established focus on electric power. The program not only responds directly to the overall balance of payments problems experienced by Third World countries that import oil, but also addresses the threat posed to development prospects by world oil depletion. To achieve the largest possible results, the World Bank has accepted the role of a catalyst and de facto guarantor of private investment. This was perhaps inevitable, since, for reasons outlined in Chapter 2, the petroleum industry has with some exceptions steered well clear of risking investments of its capital in the Third

World. (See Appendix 3, p. 131, for a description of the petroleum potential of seventy selected developing countries and the exploration activities there to date.)

Finally, although loans for production of known oil and gas reserves are fairly safe investments for a development bank (and have been available from the World Bank since 1977, the first such loan going to India), the World Bank's new willingness to finance relatively higher risk petroleum exploration activity signals an increased acceptance of responsibilities that could not have been undertaken by an institution limited by conservative banking principles. This new attitude is underlined by the fact that most of the World Bank's money will support the activities of existing national oil companies in the Third World. It should also be noted, however, that most of the preproduction lending will be in appraisal drilling (i.e., drilling after initial discovery of an oil field) and in geological and geophysical surveys and engineering.

For the developed donor countries, the meaning of the World Bank's large effort is illuminated by its history. In September 1976 U.S. Treasury Secretary William Simon wrote to Bank President Robert S. McNamara about the need for an IBRD program to support the exploitation of all minerals including oil, in the developing countries. Simon said the United States believed that "new forms of investment are needed to overcome the mutual reluctance of investors and host governments" and that the World Bank should "play a fundamental role in this effort, mobilizing funds from private and public sources, acting as intermediary between private investors and host governments, and linking private and public efforts by providing cross-guarantees of performance."[8]

Early in 1979 media reports suggested that the petroleum industry had applied considerable pressure to the U.S. Treasury, aimed at preventing U.S. support for the World Bank's program. *The New York Times* quoted Exxon's chairman as writing to Secretary Blumenthal that World Bank financing for exploration should only be made available "after ensuring the acreage involved had first been offered to industry on reasonable terms. Otherwise, the Bank's loans might only be replacing already available risk capital."[9] The history and extent of industry's influence on this matter is unclear at best. It may have had some impact in defining the scale of the Bank's program, but more likely it simply helped to focus the Bank's attempts to concentrate in areas that will not duplicate private investment.

The reasons for industry's hesitation to explore in less developed countries have already been discussed. The essential point, where donor country interests (and indeed the interests of *all* major oil importers) come to light, is the distinction between *large* new fields, which would certainly attract immediate interest from the major oil companies, and *smaller fields, whose impact on world oil supply and price would be indirect and cumulative.* The scale of recent discoveries in Mexico, for example, highlighted the potential for fossil fuel recovery in developing countries. But although the entry of a potential major exporter into the world market has great significance for major consuming countries, an equally significant breakthrough may be the recovery of previously unexploited or undiscovered reserves for domestic use in many developing countries on a comparatively small scale.

The World Bank estimates that as many as thirty-five oil-importing countries have reserves sufficient to make a "very significant" difference in the availability of oil for their own domestic consumption. But even very extensive production in only one or two of these countries would probably not affect availability of oil elsewhere in the world. So, from the perspective of Western self-interest, *the importance of the World Bank's program is to ensure that a large number of these countries become oil producers as soon as possible.* That in turn points directly to the need for a large and aggressive exploration program.

Under the World Bank's existing plans, the total new program will be at least as high as $1.2 billion by 1983:

> The proposed Bank lending program, rising to $1,500 m. (current dollars) five years from now would include $1,230 m. for oil and gas projects. About 60 percent of the lending would be for production facilities and would cover up to 20 percent of the total cost. The balance would be for preproduction activities, contributing a larger share of the costs, perhaps two-thirds on average. The total cost of the projects assisted by the Bank in FY '83 would be in excess of $4 billion. Bank-financed projects for oil and gas development would thus represent a substantial share of the upstream investment requirements of the non-OPEC developing countries in the sector.[10]

And it is likely, as mentioned above, that even this large effort will be doubled. The World Bank clearly envisions that its catalytic role will be greater for *production* projects (which are expected to attract 80 percent private investment) than for *exploration* projects (which are expected to attract 33 percent private investment), although the Bank's paper also observes that "it is very difficult at this stage to forecast the demand for Bank financing of exploratory drilling and therefore to estimate the amount of lending for this purpose."

It is not clear whether the Bank's analysts regard this as an *ade-*

quate level of investment in exploration activities, and the limits of managerial and institutional capabilities may make a larger program problematic. But the idea that the "investment requirements" of the oil-importing developing countries can be measured is somewhat misleading. The ability of these countries to absorb investment can itself be enhanced by aid programs that build technical and managerial skills. In short, it is difficult not to conclude that the World Bank's program is tailored, in part, to the likely availability of funds (the Bank's paper does not touch this question) and the anticipated range of complementary activities of other aid programs. These factors in turn are closely tied to Western and OPEC priorities for allocation of financial resources for energy development.

Finally, in the justified enthusiasm over new efforts to help Third World countries find and produce oil, it ought not to be overlooked that it will be difficult to coordinate these activities with the overall development needs of Third World populations. A very small proportion of Third World populations use the great bulk of oil- or gas-produced energy and also receive most of the benefits of other petroleum products. There is no easy way out of this dilemma. It is certainly recognized by the World Bank, which hopes that new jobs in the petroleum industries of the Third World will be an important secondary benefit of its new program. But one of the greatest gaps in development agency energy work still to be remedied, and indeed in development philosophy generally, is the almost total failure to carry out broad energy planning that considers the overall relationship between commercial energy used by the modern sector of the economy and traditional fuel used by the mass of people. One or two energy studies commissioned by these institutions have been exceptions, but with the advent of lending for petroleum projects it would seem to be increasingly important to ascertain the distribution of benefits from such new energy programs.

Institutional Cooperation

The third new area of energy activity taking shape at the World Bank is a rather grudging acceptance that it is the only existing institution capable of galvanizing other major banks and agencies and providing leadership among them. It has very recently begun to sponsor informal meetings of aid agencies that have energy assistance programs. This process, if continued, may solve the dilemma of the bilateral aid programs, which would like to continue the work of the MacPhail Group but find it politically difficult to do so.

The first meeting called by the World Bank (Paris, June 1979) discussed fossil fuels programs. The Bank's principal interest was to explain and launch its oil and gas program. Other meetings may soon be planned for different topics. At the 1979 United Nations Conference on Science and Technology for Development, the World Bank representative said:

> The Bank intends to convene a meeting to consider how research on renewable energy sources might be coordinated, priorities defined, and resources for the purpose increased, and what kind of assistance is necessary to translate research results into pilot operations and subsequently into full-scale implementation.[11]

Such a meeting would be valuable, because it would provide an opportunity for candid discussion of the overall strategy and direction of renewable energy aid. Regular consultation is also needed because it enables bilateral agencies (Western and OPEC) and multinational institutions to exchange technical information and share different approaches to energy aid projects. A formal arrangement is almost certainly needed, perhaps on the consultative group model that has worked well in other areas.

It might even be possible to utilize existing donor consortia, which, although not organized along sectoral lines, could in their annual meetings have a special focus *at the working level* on energy. At the moment, donor consortia, usually chaired by the World Bank, meet annually for twenty-two countries.[g] Regional development banks and U.N. agencies are also present. These sessions allow an opportunity for donors to examine short-term developmental constraints and to give the recipient an understanding of the level of donor activity they might expect in the following year. Representatives at donor consortia are usually high-level officials who have little knowledge of the detail associated with projects in a particular country. Hence this system would have to be adapted to provide for expert panels, with enough time and resources to do a thorough job analyzing the energy needs of the country.

A second urgent task for aid donor cooperation is to share the vast bulk of energy information gathered by aid agency project and mission teams. So much is known, though it is at present shared to such a limited extent that the "data gap" on Third World energy may not be nearly so severe as is generally presumed.

There have been important initiatives in other international and regional organizations. OLADE has sponsored the preparation of a

---

[g]Bangladesh, Burma, Korea, India, Indonesia, Nepal, Pakistan, Philippines, Thailand, Turkey, Egypt, Ghana, Kenya, Nigeria, Sahel, Sudan, Tanzania, Uganda, Zaire, Zambia, Bolivia, and the Caribbean region.

Latin American Action Plan for the Development and Massive Application of Non-Conventional Sources of Energy. Prepared with the help of the United Nations, the plan was presented to a regional meeting of Latin American energy ministers in late 1979. This program is buttressed by the efforts of the Organization of American States, for example, which in late 1978 sponsored a six-week training seminar for energy policymakers from seventeen Latin American countries. The seminar analyzed some of the available methods for performing energy supply and demand projections and long-range energy planning, and it also discussed the prospects for utilization of alternative energy sources in Latin America.

Most of the U.N. system's efforts for the next two years will be in preparation for its 1981 Conference on New and Renewable Sources of Energy. A series of preparatory technical panels and workshops are being convened in 1980, to share state-of-the-art information on solar, wind, biomass, and other sources. The work of these panels ought to define the realistic boundaries of technical choices, so that political negotiation at the conference itself can be forced to avoid the usual pitfalls of unrealistic demands and arbitrary responses. The technical panels provide a good, perhaps unique, opportunity to highlight the advantages of new energy sources and to dispel excessive expectations; in short, to do the technical homework in such a way that the benefits of cooperation are evident, indeed compelling to all.

Inevitably, the question arises—and will be debated heatedly before and during the conference—whether a new global energy institution must be established. As a whole, the U.N. system carries out a wide variety of energy-related projects, but most of these are research or educational activities. Only the International Atomic Energy Agency, based in Vienna, has an exclusive mandate within the U.N. system, focusing as it does on the promotion and regulation of nuclear power. This general lack of direction occasionally leads outside commentators to look for a central energy agency within the U.N. family, or a vesting of overall energy responsibilities in the IAEA or perhaps UNIDO. It seems highly unlikely, unfortunately, that such reorganization could avoid carrying with it the seeds of nuclear or industrial bias. Indeed, a recent attempt by the IAEA to absorb the U.N.'s very modestly staffed Centre for Natural Resources, Energy and Transport was widely opposed on these grounds, since the only non-nuclear energy planning assistance available from the U.N. system comes from this agency.

Recent history suggests that any new energy agency would incorporate all of the bitter divisions that have separated North and South on energy since 1973. Indeed, those divisions render its creation unlikely, if not impossible. It seems far sounder to encourage the quiet technical discussions that have taken place in the last few years in lieu of debates about the need for an international energy institute and to plan needed technical functions within appropriate existing organizations (for example, a great deal of research on energy conservation opportunities for developing countries in the context of industrial development and innovation could most logically be pursued by UNIDO).

Moving Ahead

None of the development assistance agencies active in the field of energy is clearly on a wrong track. Indeed, the effort to apply new energy sources, and to use traditional ones more efficiently, is so new for developing country application that it would surely be a grave mistake for aid programs to commit themselves to precise courses of action to the exclusion of a range of experimental approaches. But unfortunately, innovative thinking about existing and future energy programs has not been widespread. An exception is the World Bank's new petroleum program (and efforts to finance special funds elsewhere, particularly at UNDP, to carry out parallel efforts). Many agencies still seem more concerned to make a public fuss about their great concern over energy than to rethink and restructure their programs. There is clearly an acutely heightened interest in the problem of improving energy assistance to Third World countries, but its priority among all the other efforts of development agencies is not yet clear.

Most aid agencies have simply not conceived an energy policy that corresponds to their changing views on development as a whole. These agencies face substantial pressure to give or lend more money for energy programs, and to concentrate it in obviously needy areas such as Sahelian Africa. But none of them has really examined the energy requirements for different patterns of rural development, for example, even though they are promoting some of these patterns. Many of the traditional, unspoken assumptions still need to be questioned, urgently and comprehensively.

Development assistance for energy ought to respond to at least three types of energy needs in Third World countries. First, life-sustaining energy supplies for tasks such as cooking and minimal agricultural irrigation, and in some regions heating must be secured. Second, energy for modernizing and improving quality of life is needed to perform such tasks as medical refrigeration, improved cooking and heating, and powering of educational radio or television.

Third, increased energy supplies and improved energy productivity are needed for the modern-sector economies of developing countries. Different types of projects clearly are appropriate for each of these three jobs.

Energy assistance is more likely to succeed if designed to achieve goals that are more carefully defined than has generally been the case in many aid programs. Two complementary types of programs are possible. One type seeks to redirect the structural path of development in order to improve quality of life with less energy use—for example, by stemming urban migration, planning land and resource exploitation, and emphasizing economic growth of an energy-conserving nature. The second approach has to alter energy use directly by increasing the utilization of indigenous or renewable resources, altering energy conversion or end-use technologies, and overcoming institutional barriers to more efficient energy investments. The first type of program assumes influence over social and political circumstances in developing countries, which external donors and lenders can influence only indirectly, principally by providing better analytical and planning capability. The second type of program is more technical and probably easier to address through development assistance programs.

Large development assistance institutions are not fully able to oversee the many small experimental and demonstration projects that are needed to select the best techniques and programs. But a bigger stumbling block will be their inability, once successful approaches have been identified by such projects, to assist in their commercialization (a process that can only occur if the people who could use new energy technologies are able or helped to afford them). National and local credit institutions, which can facilitate the acquisition of alternative energy systems by those users who cannot now afford to purchase sufficient quantities of commercial energy, are going to need increased administrative and financial assistance from major donors and lenders.

The financial viability of an alternative energy system depends upon the rate of return on the investment (from enhanced output) and the costs of competing sources of energy. The first is heavily influenced by interest rates for loans and the second by the price of petroleum fuels or firewood. An advantage of equal importance to financial inability, from the standpoint of donor and recipient nations, if not the individual users, should be more rapidly decreasing prices of renewable energy systems, decreasing imports of oil, and preservation of forests. In order to make renewable energy technology transfers sustainable, programs to improve their financial

viability through soft credit, and purchasing and operating coopera-
tives, may be as important as their technical merits.

The financial mechanisms and institutions to deliver these services
do not now exist in many developing countries, although those
developed for other programs, such as agricultural assistance, may be
adaptable to the purpose. Developing these institutions and mechanisms should be a priority of energy assistance efforts to no less
degree than energy planning or research. Unfortunately, this aspect
of energy assistance has been largely ignored, even though much
hardware is now ready for dissemination and the financial obstacles
will not be removed quickly, on the theory that the ongoing hardware
development phases must precede marketing or financing phases.

The major aid agencies have not worked nearly closely enough
with two types of intermediaries: small, locally oriented private
voluntary organizations, and local institutions and development
banks that can distribute concessional funds to entrepreneurs,
promising industries, and locally designed and carried out research
work. In particular, the aid programs of some OPEC countries would
probably find it more attractive to finance lines of credit to local development banks (which can, in turn, lend to domestic manufacturers and users of renewable energy technologies), than to channel
funds indirectly into American and European companies experimenting with the new energy technologies. Ironically, OPEC efforts
to pursue this approach are somewhat hampered by the original
mandates of these local banks, which were in many cases set up with
the help of western donors.

Apart from these considerations, in their new enthusiasm to support energy programs, development agencies should not lose sight of
the fact that principal responsibility to devise and carry out new
energy programs remains with Third World governments. This is a
topic we discuss in Chapter 5. Here, we only emphasize that aid
programs will not solve Third World energy problems. The role of
Northern agencies should be to make available the types of resources—capital, technical knowledge, planning and management
capabilities—that will help the energy-poor countries of the South
to help themselves.

NOTES

1. See Commission of the European Communities, *Solar Energy for Development*, proceedings of the International Conference held at Varese, Italy,
March 26-29, 1979 (The Hague: Martinus Nijhoff, 1979).

2. Organization for Economic Cooperation and Development, 1978 *Development Cooperation Review* (Paris: OECD, 1978), table A.12, p. 203.

3. Public letter dated April 19, 1978, from Senators Percy, Case, Javits, Hart, Glenn, Metzenbaum, and Church (all of the Senate Foreign Relations Committee) to Secretary of State Vance, Secretary of Energy Schlesinger, AID Administrator Gilligan, and Office of Management and Budget Director McIntyre.

4. Netherlands Ministry of Foreign Affairs, *Development Cooperation and the World Economy* (The Hague: Government of the Netherlands, 1979), p. iv-v.

5. United Nations Conference on Trade and Development, *Financial Solidarity for Development—Efforts and Institutions of the Members of OPEC,* TD/B/627, (New York: United Nations, 1977), p. 7.

6. Efrain Friedmann, "Energy Activities of the World Bank," *Natural Resources Forum* 3, no. 1 (October 1978).

7. See World Bank, *Energy in the Developing Countries,* (Washington, D.C.: World Bank, 1980).

8. Letter from U.S. Secretary of the Treasury William E. Simon to Robert S. McNamara, dated September 30, 1976. Reprinted with permission.

9. "World Bank Spurs Energy Aid," *The New York Times,* August 22, 1979. Copyright 1979 by the New York Times Company. Reprinted by permission.

10. World Bank, *A Program to Accelerate Petroleum Production in the Developing Countries,* (Washington, D.C.: World Bank, 1979), p. 29. Reprinted by permission.

11. Statement to the United Nations Conference on Science and Technology for Development by Shirley Boskey, director, International Relations Department, World Bank, August 27, 1979. Reprinted by permission.

 *Chapter 4*

Solar Power: Can Everyone Profit?

A substantial and growing solar industry has emerged in France, the United States, Germany, and elsewhere. In the last several years multinational companies as well as small entrepreneurial enterprises have begun to look with great interest at potential markets in the Third World. Because of the large investment and potential profit at stake and the possibilities for direct industrial cooperation (or collision) between North and South, the export activity of this private sector is likely to have more eventual influence on the renewable energy future of the Third World—for good or ill—than all of the well-intentioned programs of aid agencies combined.

The solar industry is not, of course, alone in the renewable energy field in promoting its products for transfer from North to South.[a] But this industry *is* unique in one respect: Unlike biomass, small-scale hydro, and other "new" systems, solar technology is believed by its promoters to be widely applicable to both developed and developing country energy needs. Much of the basic technology—a solar collector or a photovoltaic cell, for example—could be the same everywhere, although its adaptation and application will vary (and its rapid obsolescence may create special problems for Third World

[a]For purposes of this chapter, discussion of the solar industry focuses on its concentration, in industrialized countries, on thermal and photovoltaic products. Many renewable energy sources, of course, ultimately derive from the sun, but most of these receive scant attention from the private sector in the North. Wind and biomass energy, for example, has not yet given rise to any significant industrial activity aimed at Third World markets.

investors). This chapter, therefore, focuses exclusively on the solar industry and on governmental efforts to promote sales in the Third World, because it is in this field that the potential for North-South cooperation is thought to be greatest.

A great deal of anticipation is engendered by possible solar applications in developing countries. Literature and studies have appeared in quantity, mostly in Northern countries, arguing that solar energy's earliest commercial successes should be expected for the Third World, because, for remote applications, both diesel generators and electric grid extensions are more expensive in developing country circumstances.[1] (This is particularly true when maintenance costs are considered; for example, the breakdown rate of remotely located diesel generators is so frequent that two generators often need to be installed.) In theory, utilization of decentralized solar power matches well with the needs of outlying settlements and villages that are not connected to electric power grids.

In aid agency energy programs, the prevailing attitude toward this potential is still, as we have seen, largely to await—rather than to attempt to hasten—its fulfillment. Multilateral agencies in particular have been unwilling to modify their lending criteria to suit the solar industry, nor have they sought to influence the industry's evolution toward developmental objectives. It is clear that the hesitant approach of development agencies in no way discourages the eager research and promotion of private industry, although smaller companies may be incapable of unsupported marketing in the Third World. It is certainly too soon to say with certainty that Northern solar technology is an appropriate form of North-South energy cooperation. But an export industry still at the takeoff stage, which looks as though it will have a major impact in developing countries, is more sensitive now to suggestion and guidance than it will ever be again.

Why do industry's expectations differ from those of developers? So far, the solar energy industry has produced only one product (water-heating systems) that has successfully found a mass market in their home countries. Other products—for example, those that use photovoltaic cells—cannot yet compete with conventionally powered alternatives, except for very limited remote applications such as telecommunication relay stations. The industry needs interim markets to generate sales at today's higher prices, because an increase in sales makes bulk manufacturing possible, and hence lowers costs. The need for these markets—and the possibility of subsidized purchases through aid programs—has naturally focused industry attention on Third World sales opportunities.

These possibilities are viewed with suspicion by many developing countries, on the grounds that the "terms of transfer" of the new solar technology will be unfavorable, if not oppressive, to the recipient country. They argue that the products are not being designed with development goals in mind, that hardware rather than know-how will be transferred, and that eventually yet another example of Southern dependence on Northern technology will result. There is also, as we have seen, the general suspicion that solar energy is a "second-class" technology, and only being offered as a way of conserving oil for Northern consumption. These questions arise in a larger context of resentment: The profit-making motives of private companies are sometimes assumed to be unavoidably incompatible with the developmental needs of Third World energy users.

There can be little question, if one looks to recent history, that promotion of energy technology transfer is a minefield for the promoter, buyer, and seller alike. The nuclear industry, for example, has received enormous governmental subsidies on an international scale. As noted earlier, throughout the 1960s sales of reactors to developing countries were expected to be very large. Whether or not a bright future exists for nuclear power in the Third World, it is now clear that it was folly to advocate prematurely the direct transfer of energy systems designed with developed country needs in mind (if only because most developing country electricity grids cannot absorb the power output of commercially available reactors). Impossible expectations were raised, a very genuine dependence was vigorously promoted, and comparatively little has so far been accomplished.

If those who hold the different points of view on the solar energy industry mentioned above continue on their present course, failing to make reasonable adjustments in their expectations of one another, then future disappointments are inevitable. Solar energy does offer immense potential benefits to developing countries. But it is not beyond the proven capacity of both suppliers and recipients to squander this opportunity through a mixture of excessive expectations and unreasonable demands. These could indefinitely postpone a potentially successful venture in North-South cooperation.

THE SOLAR INDUSTRIES' THIRD WORLD OBJECTIVES

Several Third World countries have found themselves besieged by solar age peddlers, both in international scientific and technical forums and through promotional efforts of individual companies. At the 1979 International Solar Energy Society (ISES) meeting in Atlanta, Georgia, and at the 1979 Conference on Solar Energy for Development sponsored by the European Community in Varese, Italy, the view that private manufacturers are gearing up for Third World markets was reaffirmed. Many developing countries are being approached directly by large firms—mostly French, German, American, and Dutch—which are busy collecting marketing data on possible sales opportunities.

At the present time U.S. manufacturers are most vigorously promoting photovoltaic cells. Two of the major American competitors, Arco Solar and Solarex, have been selling the bulk of their solar cell production internationally.[2] The French firm Sofretes, on the other hand, has already promoted in twenty-five countries solar irrigation pumps that use solar thermal collectors. In the United States, thirty-eight Fortune 500 companies are carrying out research on photovoltaic cells, while nine of the Nouvel Economiste 500 are doing so in France. Eight of these American firms and three of the French have photovoltaic products in production.[b] One major entrant in the field—the Dutch multinational Philips—is still committing large research sums to solar thermal processes for Third World application.

The industry has experienced rapid growth in sales in the last several years, but its character has changed drastically as large competitors have entered the field. For the American industry, domestic tax credits and federal buying programs have helped boost many small and medium-sized firms with sales of goods most appealing to the newly "energy-conscious" consumer, although, not surprisingly, many industry representatives characterize these subsidies as inade-

[b]U.S. companies involved in photovoltaic research (R) and production (P): American Cyanamid (R), ARCO Solar (Atlantic Richfield) (R, P), Bell Telephone Labs (R), Bausch and Lomb (R), Communications Satellite (R), Corning Glass (R), Dow Corning (R), Dupont (R), Eastman Kodak (R), Solar Power Corporation (Exxon) (R, P), Ford Motor (R), General Dynamics (R), General Electric (R), General Telephone & Electronics (R), Gould (R), Honeywell (R), Spectrolab (Hughes Aircraft), (R, P), IBM (R), Photon Power (Libby-Owens-Ford) (R, P), Litton (R), Lockheed (R), McGraw-Edison (R, P), Martin Marietta (R, P), J.V. Tyco Labs (Mobil) (R), Monsanto Chemical (R), Motorola (R, P), North American Philips (R), Northrup (R), Penwalt (R), RCA (R), Rockwell International (R), SES Systems (Shell) (R, P), TRW (R), Texas Instruments (R), Union Carbide (R), Westinghouse (R), Xerox (R), Varian (R).

French companies involved in photovoltaic cell research (R) and production (P): Photon Power (CFP) (R, P), Novelerge (CGE) (R), CIPEL (CGE) (R), France Photon (Leroy Somer) (R, P), Radiotechnique (Philips) (R, P), Rhône Poulenc (R), SNEA (R), Thomson Brandt (R), Wonder (R).

Source: Denise Cavard and Patrick Criqui, "La Stratégie des Pays Industrialisés en Matière de Développement de l'Energie Solaire: Etude Comparée Etats Unis–France" (paper for Conférence de L'Energie Nucléaire aux Nouvelles Sources d'Energie: Vers un Nouvel Ordre Energétique International, at CREDIMI, Dijon, France, March 1979), annexes II and III. (Mimeo.)

quate. The entry of large firms has injected new vigor into many of the more complex (and more centralized) uses of solar power. The fact that large firms in both the energy industry (oil, electric companies) and elsewhere (aerospace, chemicals, electronics) are moving into control or partial control of solar companies can hardly be ignored. Nearly every major U.S. oil company—and two of the leading European-based firms—now owns or controls a large share of a solar company.[c]

These developments combine with the emphasis of government research budgets on "big solar" (see Chapter 2) to turn the industry away from the type of research and development that might produce technology most readily transferable to the Third World. Research on power towers, solar satellites, and synthetic fuel naturally receives attention because solar electricity that is centrally generated would fit most easily into the existing power distribution systems of industrialized countries. Simpler programs that emphasize decentralized systems took root in the small entrepreneurial sector, and have therefore been relatively neglected by government research priorities. This is not to say that substantial research and progress is not being made in these areas (flat-plate water heating and passive architectural designs have made impressive gains both in efficiency and in the lowering of price); it is only to indicate that the focus of Northern country exporters has been influenced by the types of research subsidies provided by European and American governments. This tendency toward standardized products that are marketable on a scale profitable for large enterprises limits the range of product choices available to potential Third World buyers. As one Third World observer at the Atlanta ISES Conference remarked, "Much of the hardware on display is far too expensive for our needs . . . and many times it is not applicable to our particular situation."[3]

French and German motives for supporting their solar industries are rather different. The climate of Northern Europe makes many solar applications a remote possibility in Germany, so the German effort is therefore primarily, not secondarily, motivated by the search for export opportunities. (And as we discuss below, this focus has alerted German exporters to the benefits of a cooperative outlook; German solar exports seem better regarded in the Third World than either French or American efforts.) The French government has all of these factors to bear in mind, but also wants to nurture a grow-

[c]A partial listing includes: ARCO: Northrup, ARCO Solar; Exxon: Day-Star, Solar Power; Gulf: General Atomic; Mobil: J.V. Tyco Laboratories; Shell: SES; Amoco: Solarex; CFP: Sofretes (French) and Photon Power (USA); and ELF Aquitaine: GIF.

ing source of employment in France that relies on close cooperation with former colonies. As recently stated by the Minister of Industry, French solar policy "should not only strengthen the country's autonomy with regard to energy, but should develop a new field of activities angled toward foreign markets and that will provide new industrial employment."

APPROACHES TO THIRD WORLD
SOLAR PROJECTS

The motives of an industry, or of a government that promotes that industry, are often the target of Third World criticism, as though motives of Northern self-interest (profit, job-creation, market opportunities) eradicate the possibility of real benefits for developing countries. But must this always be so? Is it not possible for Southern buyers (and the aid agencies that often finance their purchases) to influence the solar industry toward their own ends, in effect guiding would-be exporters to do business geared to development needs? Because the solar industry is young and crowded, many competitors will fail. Third World buyers and development-financing agencies need ways of ensuring that the successful Northern exporters will be those that cooperate most closely with them to develop and adapt solar technology geared to their particular needs.

This is a difficult but not impossible task. It is unfortunately made more difficult by the current emphasis of those aid institutions that have shown some interest in solar energy and already subsidized solar sales in the Third World. The widespread concern for the plight of the extremely poor Sahelian countries has created a substantial interest in funding solar opportunities there. These projects are easily justified by the focus of many donors and lenders on the "poorest of the poor." Although the value of such projects for exciting interest and governmental support in host countries is significant, a strong case can also be made that better opportunities for utilizing solar energy are to be found in locations where farmers and villagers have an income large enough—with the support of rural credit schemes—to facilitate their own purchase of solar energy products. Commercialization, and therefore widespread distribution and use, can only occur when the benefits of a solar purchase allow buyers an economic advantage over using available alternatives.

One project that has been designed with immediate commercialization in mind is currently being negotiated between an American solar firm (Solar Electric International) and the government of India. The company hopes to begin partially subsidized sales on a mass scale of a small portable water pump powered by photovoltaic cells. The pump has been designed primarily for use in the local circumstances: A portable pump is needed during the daylight hours to transfer river or canal water to the plots of small farmers. A great deal of power is not needed, even for wells, because these river basin holdings benefit from a high water table. After an initial high-cost production start, the pump will be priced to attract customers who were unable to afford conventional water pumping. Finally, the company has worked directly with Indian institutions and has agreed to shift large portions of its manufacturing and servicing facilities to India. Despite these apparent advantages, however, the project has been stalled by opposition to import licenses resulting from the lobbying of the Indian solar industry. Their research may be sufficiently advanced to be competitive, but their marketing has left them far behind. Hence, the Indian scientific community is eager to protect its indigenous solar industry, even at the expense of a potentially valuable project.

Perhaps more projects have not appeared along these lines because, under today's circumstances, most would-be exporters feel they have no choice but to go where the money is; thus, they are largely promoting projects for Africa, with the hope that development aid agencies will provide purchasing power. An example of this aid-oriented project development is the solar thermal pump project jointly funded by the French and American aid agencies in Bakel, Senegal. The project resulted from the efforts of one company (Thermo-Electron), which shaped the location of the solar unit, the type of technology used, and the timing of the project. Host government participation (through a management and infrastructure support group, SINAES) is only marginal, although Thermo-Electron seems to understand the impact that many of those energy systems could have on village life and seems, philosophically at least, not to be opposed to government participation in most aspects of the design and manufacturing process.

A third type of project involves "cooperation," rather than "aid," between two governments who are supposed to share responsibilities, costs, and benefits. The German Ministry for Research and Technology seeks out such projects—for example, in India and Egypt, where it has sponsored experimental solar power stations. The U.S. Department of Energy also uses this approach, under its program of Technical Cooperation Agreements. A $100 million deal with Saudi Arabia (the costs are shared equally between the two governments) primarily involves the transfer of "high technology" photovoltaic systems to a model solar village in Saudi Arabia. Although this project will create a certain demand for solar products, that is a relatively minor impact. The importance of this project is its opening of the solar field to cooperation with Middle Eastern oil producers. These countries are definitely interested in establishing a relationship with the United States solar industry (through governmental sponsorship). In addition to Saudi Arabia, Kuwait, Qatar, the United Arab Emirates, and Iraq all have the wealth and the interest to boost solar technology transfers on a vast scale. Of course, this particular project's replicability would be questionable in countries that lack discretionary wealth, but there are applications in the project other than photovoltaics (solar heating and cooking, desalinization, and agricultural systems) that might well be applicable in various countries. (See Appendix 2, p. 129 for details on the United States/Saudi solar agreement).

PROMOTION OF THE SOLAR INDUSTRY

Official French and American support for the solar industry springs from different attitudes. But neither seems prepared, at least yet, to promote Third World development objectives by suggesting to industry that it adopt new types of business ventures with developing countries. It is harder to characterize the West German government's approach, although some German deals seem to strike a satisfactory balance between industry and host government objectives.

American arrangements to promote solar exports, though in theory diffused throughout several departments of the U.S. government, are in practice largely placed in the Department of Energy. The Department of Commerce, the National Energy Research Laboratories, the Solar Energy Research Institute, the Export-Import Bank, and the Overseas Private Investment Corporation all theoretically have something to do with the process, but no notable efforts have yet been mounted. The Department of Energy has focused on the development of photovoltaic exports under the 1978 Solar Photovoltaic Energy Research Development and Demonstration Act.[d] It chairs an interagency Solar Commercialization Working

---

[d]DOE's major involvement has been the preparation during 1979 of an "International Photovoltaics Program Plan" required under the Solar Photovoltaic Energy Research, Development, and Demonstration Act. The Solar Energy Research Institute is the national laboratory that carried out this task. In this plan, developmental objectives were subordinated to promotional mechanisms. *Conceptually,* the *approach* to devising this plan was deficient in at least four respects:

1. The congressional mandate for the study did not embrace renewable energy technologies other than photovoltaics. Uncritical emphasis on only one type

Group, which concentrates its efforts on three fronts—contacts with private U.S. investors and industry, liaison with officials in other U.S. agencies and multilateral organizations, and approaches to foreign governments and foreign commercial interests. This group seems so far to be ineffectual, not so much because any particular individual or group of individuals is at fault, but rather because the mandate originally given the group (to assess worldwide "solar potential") is much too broad, and funds for demonstration and other programs have not been available. U.S. industry has found neither the market assessment help that it would like, nor any government export promotion commitment to set up the demonstrations and trade fairs that it deems essential to compete with the French effort.

On the whole, the French government has developed a more sophisticated apparatus to support its solar industry than has the United States. To a large extent, these arrangements were covered in Chapter 3: They arise from the close links between French companies and the French aid program. The French government has sponsored several solar market surveys in Africa and through a consulting firm has encouraged innovative methodological work (for example, an economic study of cost-benefit analysis for solar energy projects may be undertaken).

The Commissariat à l'Energie Atomique not only owns a majority interest in Sofretes, but it also controls the major windpower manufacturer, Aerowatt. This highly centralized structure assures the French solar industry of finance, as well as technical and research

---

of renewable energy technology would probably create a market distortion and result in the application of photovoltaic cells to tasks that might be more economically served by some other renewable power source (wind, thermal solar, biogas, and so on) or by an improvement in the efficiency with which conventional power sources (wood, kerosene) are used.
2. More attention was paid to *market* development than to *country* development. The two are not necessarily at odds with each other but can easily be (as past experiences have proven). At a time when governments are grappling with the issues of the New International Economic Order—in particular the problem of terms of technology transfer—it seems senseless to initiate a major international effort that ignores these issues.
3. The approach assumes the widespread utility of photovoltaics, and the existence of a market, without making any attempt to analyze existing or anticipated energy uses or needs.
4. There appears to have been little concern with adapting U.S. photovoltaic technology to developing country circumstances. A large effort will be needed to adapt U.S. photovoltaic technology to the social, cultural, and climatological conditions of many developing nations. Leaving the task to industry does not ensure that loads and systems will be designed with developmental constraints in mind, nor does it encourage the export to LDCs of technical and operational know-how and manufacturing infrastucture rather than finished energy systems.

skills. There is, as a result, a self-assurance not found in most of the American companies. Although this is advantageous for the industry, it may not be entirely a good thing for purchasers, since there is little incentive in the French industry to develop products and facilities that could survive without the assured subsidy that is now available.

The West German approach to solar energy cooperation is based on the principle of identifying a cooperating institution in the receiving country to develop the project and share know-how. This work is done by the Ministry for Research and Technology, which has sponsored a number of solar energy research programs in the Third World. The German aid program (the BMZ) seems to be directing its renewable energy program toward biomass projects and is also interested in mini-hydro projects. Without direct aid program support, therefore, German solar exporters must look to close cooperation with host country institutions (the real problem with this approach is to find adequate institutions with which to work: The BMZ may be drawn increasingly into institution-building efforts).

In Egypt, for example, West German companies are collaborating with the government's solar research laboratory to design and build a ten-kilowatt solar power plant. None of the technical details are to be withheld from the Egyptians, who also expect to receive concessional support for the manufacture of the plant and some of the required components. In India, too, a West German firm Messerschmitt-Bölkow-Blohm (MBB) is carrying out a joint venture with Bharat Heavy Electricals, Ltd. (a state-owned company), to build a ten-kilowatt solar power plant to meet the energy needs of a small village. So far, each government has contributed about $1 million.

Generally speaking, the apparent willingness of the West Germans to share know-how results in a warmer welcome than many other outsiders have received in the Third World. And the official view of the Ministry for Science and Technology is that German companies cannot expect markets for renewable energy technology products except as a result of cooperative research and design that establishes a need for specific components.

So far, solar exporters have found little support in international financing institutions like the World Bank or its parallel regional organizations, although their interest is eagerly awaited (and although many solar advocates, in the U.S. Congress and elsewhere, have been pushing hard to accelerate the Bank's effort). The World Bank has only funded some research and testing projects, but has found no commercially viable solar ventures. This largely reflects the fact that economically sound solar projects are still few and far between. But it also indicates the difficulties faced by large development-financing institutions in identifying (or recognizing) opportunities that deviate too far from established practices. They have not, for example, so far devoted any resources to looking for solar projects where the physical, social, and financial circumstances come together in an economically justifiable project.

SOLAR INDUSTRY MOMENTUM

What can be done to harness the forces of profit and industrial initiative so that the solar energy industry grows in ways responsive to specific Third World development needs? It would be naive to imagine that the answer to this question can be found overnight, through a revolution in industrial cooperation and transfer between North and South. But it is possible even now to identify the broad concerns and objectives of the solar industry in the North, on the one hand, and those of developing country governments on the other. Successful transfer of solar technology will mean different things to different people. Industrial interests want to protect trade secrets and prefer to transfer mass-produced products. The greatest fear of the American solar industry, for example, is that the U.S. government will find a means of giving away proprietary information in the name of development assistance or diplomatic goodwill (concern over the U.S./Saudi solar program is a good example).

The most advanced Third World nations, such as India or Brazil, generally will not want to import solar hardware unless the deal includes close cooperative links that will assist their own competitive industries. The majority of developing countries want to obtain the benefits of research and development while contributing a minimum of scarce risk capital for product development that is appropriate to their national circumstances. (The photovoltaic industry poses a special concern for developing countries of avoiding commitment to technologies that are fast-changing and become obsolete almost overnight.) Perhaps most of all, acceptable technology transfer must include, from the Third World perspective, the acquisition of know-how and a contribution to national technological self-reliance.

The differences between these two perspectives are large, but not insurmountable. Official programs of Northern governments designed to promote solar exports to developing countries need to be reexamined in light of potential common ground. For example, licensing operations, sale of know-how, and transfer of solar manufacturing capability all need to receive higher priority than they are now given, in comparison to support for direct sales of solar hardware. Opportunities for profitable joint ventures and other manufacturers' agreements that involve the exchange of technical capabilities and information between industries and Third World producers should be actively promoted. This approach would help ease the tensions that typify technology transfer discussions. If the industrialized countries are willing to use developing country markets as a transitional mechanism for the solar industry (to refine products and expand production), this activity should perhaps be accompanied by the transfer of enough knowledge to buyers to encourage the less developed countries' own growth of solar industries.

Development agencies and Third World governments face an urgent choice: They can await industry initiatives (supported by the export-minded tendency of developed country governments), then complain later when it turns out that industry has protected its own interests but not the Third World's. Or they can try to devise new consultative processes to bring companies and Third World buyers together in order to map the boundaries of solar energy use that might best meet developmental needs while maintaining the interest and export commitment of industry.

Examples of international cooperation of this sort already exist. The Norwegian Petroleum Industry Development Company was recently established to coordinate offers of Norwegian offshore oil recovery expertise to Third World countries, in order to help them mitigate problems of bad or random technology selection due to their lack of knowledge of alternatives. The new company is a consortium of fourteen leading Norwegian businesses working in all major aspects of the petroleum industry. It operates closely with the Norwegian development assistance agency and with the national export council.

This particular example may not necessarily be relevant as a model for the solar industry. But as aid agencies' energy coordination begins to take shape, it surely must include the means to bring together the energy industry and its developing countries buyers. The German government has proposed, for example, that ways be found to start closer cooperation between industry and user countries at the earliest stages of research and development. UNIDO has suggested strengthening a few research institutions in the Third World, making them into "centers of excellence" to help countries acquire expertise in buying, producing, and adapting the new solar technologies. This sort of idea should be acted upon. In Chapter 6, some steps are suggested to set this process in motion.

NOTES

1. See, for example, Norman L. Brown and James W. Howe, "Solar Energy for Village Development," *Science* 199 (February 10, 1978): 651–57; and Louis Rosenblum, et al., *Photovoltaic Power Systems for Rural Areas of Developing Countries*, NASA Technical Memorandum 79097 (National Aeronautics and Space Administration, 1979).

2. DOE estimates that approximately half of 1978 sales of photovoltaic modules were in foreign markets. See Department of Energy, *Export Potential for P.V. Systems: Preliminary Report* (DOE, April 1979), pp. 2–3.

3. Jeff Passmore, "Politics, Technology Dominate Atlanta Solar Convention," *Canadian Renewable Energy News*, June/July 1979, p. 5.

✳ *Chapter 5*

Third World Decisionmaking: Relations With The Energy Institutions of The North

An international forum of development and energy specialists held in June 1979 provided a good platform for the airing of diverse views on what role industrialized countries should perform in helping Third World nations meet their energy needs.[a] At the end of three days' debate, two informal spokesmen emerged (one Indian and one Latin American), who summarized the views of recognized Third World experts (including those of many government officials speaking in a private capacity) in this way:

1. North-South energy cooperation cannot make real progress until the North "puts its own house in order" by drastically reducing its lion's share consumption of oil. (This argument assumes that Northern demand drives the price of oil out of the effective reach of poor countries.)

[a]The Royal Institution Forum on Third World Energy Strategies and the Role of Industrialized Countries was held in London on June 20–22, 1979. It brought together speakers from the Third World to address some crucial aspects of the problem of energy and development from a Third World viewpoint. Rather than focus on descriptions of the individual experiences of Third World countries, the conference discussed the role of the developed countries in what should be a common effort to deal with problems affecting the whole world. Also participating in the conference were a number of representatives of developed country aid agencies and research institutes. (Sponsors of the forum were the U.K. Ministry of Overseas Development, the Swedish Beijer Institute, the Atlantic Richfield Company, the Canadian International Development Research Centre, the Groupe de Bellerive, and the International Institute for Environment and Development.)

97

2. Likewise, real progress hinges on the willingness of Northern governments to pay greater attention to—and in fact "have more respect for"—the energy needs and strategies of developing countries.
3. The most badly needed help is for building up analytical, managerial and planning skills in the energy field in developing countries.

Is it possible to make progress toward fulfilling these demands? Indeed, do they serve North-South negotiation well as the basis of long-term cooperation? Northern reaction to these kinds of goals—particularly among domestic politicians, but even among diplomats—tends to dismiss them as unrealistic, rhetorical posturing. That reaction utterly fails to appreciate the depth of bitter feeling that pervades the Third World's perception of Northern energy consumption, using as it does 57.3 percent of the world's commercial energy (oil, coal, gas, nuclear, and hydroelectric) for 16.2 percent of the world's population.[1] On the other hand, Southern negotiating postures in the North-South dialogue have consistently underestimated the decisive effect of domestic politics on the international energy policies of the industrialized democracies. The purchasing power of Northern, particularly American, consumers is sufficiently flexible relative to its Southern counterparts to continue to support energy-intensive lifestyles, albeit painfully, even at higher oil prices. The interests of the voting consumer in Europe and North America are put first. Furthermore, public perceptions in industrialized countries have never favored any energy concessions to the Third World, since the public's view is that the general political alignment of these nations with OPEC—an alignment which often involves a deep sense of solidarity, based upon common historical or geopolitical experience—condemns them to suffer the consequences of higher global energy prices.

Southern energy spokesmen privately acknowledge this quandary. Indeed, most Third World nations face similar political barriers to reforming national lifestyles. Take the example of Mexico. Here the twin goals of land reform and agrarian development have proved politically difficult to achieve because the land-owning class holds the balance of political power. Thus, despite the success of land redistribution as the basis for Mexico's rapid growth in agricultural production in the 1960s, many old inequities still remain and new ones have been created (the new, sometimes illegal, "estates" of northern Mexico's irrigated areas are one example). The underlying goal of braking the overwhelming migration of rural populations into Mexico's cities was undermined by the inevitable opposition of the landholding class. It is perhaps not surprising that attacking rural poverty, the root cause of migration to the cities, continues to be political dynamite.

It is reasonable to conclude from this and many similar situations that the Third World should beware of predicating its energy expectations on unlikely shifts in the domestic politics of Northern nations, as well as that Northern development aid planners should refrain from thinking they can dictate internal political realignment in the South. In many countries, energy aid planners with new ideas face the barrier of an entrenched Third World elite (whose existence is never mentioned in the debates of the North-South dialogue) who have adopted a Western lifestyle. Their resistance to change holds at least as much sway in their own countries as the commitment of consumers in the North to an oil-rich way of life. Aid agencies are no better placed to dismantle this elite than the Third World is to force the industrialized countries to put their own energy economy in order.

The rhetorical flourishes of strategic political demands may have some psychological impact. However, it seems hopelessly counterproductive for Third World spokesmen to portray them as non-negotiable prerequisites to immediate action. Indeed, such confrontational tactics probably only detract from the importance of the third priority noted above, that Third World nations most need energy assistance in building up their own decisionmaking and planning capacity.

WHO MAKES AID AGENCY ENERGY POLICY?

Aid agencies generally take refuge behind the claim that their programs and projects are created in response to the requests of developing countries. In the realm of energy, in particular, this is far from the whole story. For example, the World Bank's new oil and gas program, described in Chapter 3, and the international momentum gathering behind it resulted from donor nation and development agency initiatives. The new interest in renewable energy shares similar ancestry, traceable to the Bonn summit.

In the field of energy, donor governments do not necessarily expect developing countries to take the initiative, because both sides know that many aid-receiving nations, particularly the poorest of the oil-importing countries, lack the technical and institutional capacity to do so. In Mali, for example, the renewable energy projects of both the European Development Fund and the U.S. Agency for International Development were conceived, designed, and presented to the government by outsiders. This was unavoidable if there were to be any renewable energy initiatives in Mali, since the government's solar energy laboratory desperately needs funds, trained manpower, and equipment if it is to be an effective instrument of national policy. Even with extensive outside support, the priorities for allocation of resources would have to be questioned: In the Sahelian region, for example, there are three solar energy laboratories sponsored by national governments, carrying out research that seems marginally useful, in some cases, to the immediate needs of the countries. There is a coordinating mechanism of the Sahelian governments and outside agencies, the Permanent Inter-State Committee for Drought Control in the Sahel (CILSS), but it was most effective during the period of aid to relieve the suffering caused by the drought of the mid-seventies. Its focus is primarily on water and food programs, and it has so far done very little to coordinate energy research or aid programs.

In the poorest countries, energy projects tend to be identified and financed by aid agencies in the context of planning that is also largely their own work. To the extent that the poorest—and institutionally weakest—developing countries have any national energy plan whatsoever, it often seems geared to justifying aid agency investment. Up to now, the unwillingness of aid agencies to support national energy planning or to provide training programs for government personnel has meant that fairly narrow sectoral studies have been carried out in a relative vacuum of overall national energy policy. However it must be remembered that national energy planning is a quite new phenomenon in Western as well as Third World countries, and is only now taking its place alongside the recent evolution of population, agricultural and industrial policies.

More-advanced Third World nations make the significant energy planning decisions themselves, even if they rely heavily on outside expertise and finance to illuminate their choices. Both Egypt and Kenya, for example, have welcomed donor assistance to undertake major energy planning functions, but national institutions (particularly in Kenya) have worked very closely with the outside advisors. The U.S. Department of Energy's national energy assessment of Egypt has been discussed above and some deficiencies mentioned. Despite the relative sophistication of the Egyptian government's energy establishment (as compared to many Third World nations), without this intensive, rather abrupt, application of outside planning assistance it is unlikely that energy availability would have been technically recognized or politically accepted as a constraint on development. Of course, it is a glaring problem, in the Egyptian view, that a shortage of trained energy analysts creates any dependence whatever on outside judgments where such highly sensitive national priorities are concerned.

The example of Kenya is worth considering in somewhat greater detail, because its situation combines a fairly sophisticated national energy establishment, an acute awareness of deforestation problems and the possible role of renewable energy programs, and a very dangerous degree of dependence on imported oil. The Kenyan National Council for Science and Technology, working within the Ministry of Economic Planning, has a mandate to create a long-term national energy plan, integrating petroleum, electricity, and traditional fuel demand and supplies. The council sought help from the United Nations Development Programme (and the U.N.'s Centre for Natural Resources, Energy and Transport), beginning late in 1978, to undertake a national energy planning project. It included a rural energy survey, carried out by trained surveyors, who examined the existing energy-use patterns in over 4,000 households. In addition, the program also includes an attempt to establish a petroleum exploration and development policy. The ultimate objective of the entire undertaking is to make available the analytical material with which Kenya can plan a national energy policy and to help the government establish a ministry or other institution that can carry out the plan.

Discussions with government officials in Kenya reveal a clear preference for this kind of outside energy assistance, which builds up the local capability to plan and assess realistic energy options. No problem is more acute in a country like Kenya than the shortage of skilled manpower, which can be felt everywhere. The government is now seeking help with practical research and training institutes, rural energy extension services for reforestation and perhaps biogas, placement and exchange of staff in developed country institutions, and funding for specialized consultants to help in long-term planning. The role of development assistance agencies in this scenario is still being defined. The critical function, which can only be fulfilled by a national government, is to coordinate the various outsider activities and shape them into an effective program. Without strong governmental direction, the implementation of energy projects may not be adequately linked to energy policy planning, and energy policy itself may be divorced from national development planning.[2]

In the most administratively and technologically advanced Third World nations, such as Brazil, India, or Argentina, the planning and decisionmaking role of outside agencies is almost incidental, entirely subordinated to the national "politics of energy." In India, for example, in 1979 the government shifted allocation of national resources in favor of subsidizing rural needs (including renewed emphasis on traditional energy-light cottage industries) and away from energy-intensive industries. The new policy, if continued, could have profoundly limiting implications for the national effort to remedy the acute shortage of power for industrial production in the cities, but of course, it may also reduce the demand for commercial energy. None of these decisions, of course, has been very much affected by development assistance intervention, but the cumulative impact of the Indian decisions has the potential to affect drastically the types of projects that aid programs are asked to fund, and also eventually to reduce Indian dependence on outside investment in energy production.

DEVELOPMENT ASSISTANCE:
NEW STRATEGIES FOR
ENERGY COOPERATION

Development aid agencies and international financing institutions are increasingly aware that their traditional focus on centrally generated electricity projects has not touched most of the people in many of the countries they serve. They are also aware that a broader range of energy choices for aid-needing nations, rather than a total redirection of programs, is called for. It would be folly to suggest that aid agencies turn away from the power and fuel needs of "modern-sector" industrialized growth, not least because such a redirection would undermine the economic growth of many countries. Yet, defenders of the traditional ways of doing business in energy assistance are still so entrenched, in many cases, that charges of "bias" are often leveled by them against any proposal that favors a more open-minded outlook.

The scales are gradually being tipped by a growing awareness in many Third World nations that the transitional energy era that will move them beyond oil and the atom can be reached by alternative paths, some of which are not readily available to industrialized countries. Many developing countries believe that they can stay committed to their present development goals by moving through the fossil fuel era and only then, perhaps, following the more developed countries into the renewable energy era. Or they can choose development paths that are more realistic about the long-range fate of an oil-based existence. Some developing countries, like South Korea, Brazil, and others, are fully committed to energy-intensive growth. Others, like Mexico, have examined development alternatives but so far have found established patterns to be politically unavoidable. Many Third World nations, however, have not made irrevocable commitments to one development pattern or another. An acute awareness of certain issues, such as the importance of choosing new technologies carefully (not only for energy production, but in choices of agricultural and urban investment, modes of transport, etc.), shows that a widening process of decision-making has been politically awakened. This awakening is unlikely to produce large results until major breakthroughs occur in renewable energy sources. Since few developing countries can afford extensive experimentation, they are bound to depend upon external involvement and help.

The crossroads of energy choices lack signposts. The trend in aid agencies to emphasize "basic human needs" for the poorest has met with increasingly vocal resistance from developing country governments. It is resented as one more example of imperial tutelage that diverts scarce foreign currency, as well as national counterpart resources, away from modern-sector projects, which may accumulate savings faster and hence prepare a springboard for later rapid growth. To the extent that renewable energy programs are associated exclusively with basic human need priorities, they are unlikely to gain widespread acceptance with Third World governments (which is crucial, and should not be confused with the support of Third World academics and researchers).

At the same time, any renewable energy aid program is doomed to failure if it conveys the impression that priority for alternative energy sources has little scope in advanced industrial nations and is a strategy suitable only for "backward" countries. For aid programs to succeed, the possessors of the high-energy technologies will have to show a substantial commitment to investment in alternative energy themselves. If not, complaints about second-class technology will be impossible to refute. There continues to be considerable disagreement over the extent to which this is being done. For example, several years ago a study by the U.S. Congressional Research Service claimed that:

> The United States has by no means resolved what is at best an ambivalent policy position regarding the role and deployment of alternative energy sources within its own economy. Until this ambivalence is resolved, U.S. initiatives encouraging other nations to use alternate energies could be viewed with suspicion or could otherwise negatively influence U.S. foreign economic and other foreign assistance policies.[3]

Despite increased budgeting for alternative energy, the industrialized countries may never resolve these questions as a matter of domestic *policy*. Indeed, it is undoubtedly more important to resolve them in practice. Third World countries will continue to evaluate Western domestic energy programs very closely, looking for signs of "co-operation" in place of the "exploitation" they have perceived—rightly or wrongly—in the past.

WHO SPEAKS FOR THE THIRD WORLD?

At the outset of this chapter, it was pointed out that the diversity of developing country energy resources and needs has been widely recognized. But this complexity can be camouflaged beneath attempts to maintain political solidarity on global energy issues. The difficult responsibility of the energy aid institutions of industrialized countries is to avoid letting homogeneity undermine creative and diversified energy possibilities.

Self-appointed spokesmen for the Third World deserve no more credible response than their Northern counterparts. It is critical, therefore, to bear in mind that the needs and desires of the developing countries can *only* be identified by particular countries, *not* by spokesmen in the general setting of the North-South dialogue—and that many countries lack the institutional capacity to carry out this task effectively. When Latin American officials, for example, take the political lead in energy debates, they may overlook that their countries are generally more advanced in their energy planning activities and more committed to oil economies than are many African or Southern Asian nations. It is easy to forget that the preeminent need of the poorest countries is for honest, disinterested help with institution building. This can be jeopardized by idealistic insistence on the need to "allow" Third World nations to conceive and implement their own energy strategies. The late start of development agencies in helping the poorest countries tackle the critical problem of fuel-wood depletion, for example, is explicable in part by the fact that a few years ago neither these countries nor the agencies had trained staff available to recognize the nature of the problem, perceive its threatening implications, and carry out countermeasures.

It seems unavoidable that new energy programs and priorities will to a considerable degree be mistrusted by aid-receiving nations—and thus at least be partially undermined—so long as they are announced without real consultation by the policy planners of industrialized countries. The aid-giving nations can best assure the creation and acceptance of wider ranging energy programs in the Third World by making an all-out effort, through training and institutional support, to help developing countries shoulder responsibility for their own energy futures.

NOTES

1. World Bank, *World Development Report 1979* (Washington, D.C.: World Bank, 1979), p. 37. The developing countries, with 52.2 percent of the world's population, consume only 13.8 percent of the world's commercial energy.

2. The authors are grateful to Mr. Patrick Nyoike of the Kenya National Council for Science and Technology and to Mr. T.S. Tuschak, UNDP energy advisor to the Government of Kenya, for the clarity of their views as expressed at the Royal Institution Forum, mentioned above.

3. Excerpt from a Congressional Research Service Report on a United Nations Conference on Alternate Energy and an International Alternate Energy Commission, as reprinted in the *Congressional Record* of 95th Congress, Second Session, July 26, 1978, S. 11885.

※ *Chapter 6*

Breaking The Logjam

Two fundamental economic assumptions have recently been overthrown. Their abandonment is having a worldwide effect that is likely to be much greater than we can now envision.

The first assumption was that cheap commercial energy would be available indefinitely as a principal foundation of economic growth. The second was that *free* fuel would serve the heating and cooking needs of the world's poor (and largely rural) inhabitants. Now, firewood and oil race to outstrip one another in rates of depletion and spiraling cost. As a result, the world does not face a problem of tinkering with the old energy order; it must radically alter and indeed replace that order. So far governments and the international institutions that serve them have been unwilling or unable to meet this challenge, even though massive pressure for change is building against old inertias and resistances. Nowhere is this logjam more perplexing than in the response of Western governments toward the energy problems of the developing world, even though the logical steps that might be taken would, in most cases, serve mutual interests. It is difficult to respond technologically, because most new energy sources are still being researched and tested. It seems impossible to respond financially on an adequate scale, because "aid"— even programs instituted principally by donor self-interest—almost always lacks broad domestic political support. And it is thought naive to respond with political creativity, if the polarized North-South dialogue is a sound indicator of the willingness to compromise. This impasse is not, of course, exclusively or even primarily a result of Western inaction; rather it is perpetuated by that "suspicious triangle" described in Chapter 1.

But where does this impasse leave the West in its energy relations with the Third World? The Brandt Commission has recently highlighted the common concerns of North and South in their overall economic relations. With respect to energy, both developed and less developed countries need secure oil supplies now and for the foreseeable future. Both have a profound stake in hastening the advent of renewable energy sources, and both depend upon the security of the international financial system. The need to cooperate is becoming overwhelming. And indeed, many comparatively small practical measures have been taken or are contemplated. But their magnitude does not compare favorably to the scale of the problems they are meant to solve. They are not the product of fundamental rethinking of old assumptions about resource availability, capital flows, technological innovation, and development aid. In short, with one or two important exceptions, the recent Western response to the developing world's energy plight up to now looks too much like rearranging deck chairs on the Titanic.

GOALS FOR MUTUAL BENEFIT

As we emphasized in Chapter 1, energy aid and cooperation programs have lacked strategic focus. It is not therefore surprising that the objectives of specific programs are often ill-defined and rarely reflect any effort at setting priorities. In the first chapter we emphasized some essential elements of a strategy for energy aid and cooperation. Here we suggest five objectives to be emphasized in the new energy programs of the eighties. We believe these objectives will be politically acceptable to each side of the energy triangle. They also seek to balance efforts to alleviate immediate crises against the need to pursue longer term readjustments, and they can be designed so as to mobilize the necessary capital, technology, and organizational effort.

First, it is in the North's own interest to help finance and carry out exploration for, and production of, oil in developing countries that now import oil. The major oil exporters need have no fears as to the impact of such activity on the price of their oil. Demand for oil is such that their economic interests cannot be threatened by this kind of assistance. Indeed, to the extent that oil importing poor countries can meet their own needs, the political solidarity of the Third World is less likely to be shattered by OPEC pricing policies. This last argument might work against Western willingness to cooperate, of course, to the extent that the Western industrialized nations feel threatened by Third World alliances. But Western governments are far more interested in improving their own energy positions than in devising problematic ways of disrupting Third World solidarity.

Second, the rash of governmental programs to promote the export of solar energy technology to developing countries must be designed to avoid the pitfalls of other kinds of technology transfer and to be mutually beneficial for both solar exporters and importers. Remarkably little creativity in this regard has so far been shown by the four or five Western governments (and the European Community) who are eager to subsidize their solar industries' marketing in the Third World. New approaches are supposed to be a matter of Western self-interest because, put simply, sharing solar technology could be the West's political compensation for consuming the lion's share of the world's oil. But technology transfer programs that pay only lip service to developing country participation and indigenous capability have rarely, if ever, taken firm root. There is, therefore, a more abiding Western self-interest in encouraging genuine partnership in energy innovation.

The third objective for the eighties is closely related to the opportunities for cooperation on solar energy. Many OPEC (particularly Arab) countries have recently shown great interest in solar energy. Joint solar energy programs with oil-exporting countries not only can create new markets in those countries, but can also lead to a broadening and strengthening of support for the renewable energy effort in the poorer developing countries. Arab aid donors, in particular, recognize that they too will benefit from efforts to tap renewable energy resources in developing countries. It should therefore be a major objective of Western energy aid to work increasingly closely with the aid programs of oil-exporting countries, both to ensure that OPEC as well as Western capital is reinvested in energy and to achieve the broader political benefits of increasing cooperation with some of the OPEC members.

As a fourth objective, the disastrous depletion of world firewood supplies must be slowed, if possible halted, and indeed reversed. This may appear at first sight to require more altruism than some of the other priorities we have listed. But for those who see degradation of natural resources—and the resulting competition for those that remain—as remote from present political crises, we would point out that at least one regional war fought in the last ten years (between Ethiopia and Somalia) had as a principal cause competition for disappearing rangeland. The prospects for the poorest countries seem even more disquieting when one adds competition between use of land for food and fuel to the equation.

A fifth and final objective covers every energy aid project: Such programs have to increase their emphasis on helping developing countries to solve their own energy problems. Third World universities, research facilities, and even government agencies need financial support and technical assistance. Practically speaking, there is no alternative to such an effort: If Western donors simply descend with their own solutions, local suspicion and resistance will be insurmountable.

THE DIPLOMATIC CHALLENGES

It is relatively easy to offer objectives. It is less easy to devise a realistic path toward them. Is it possible to move toward cooperation with the major oil exporters for the benefit (in the first instance) of the poor developing countries, without simultaneously negotiating with the members of OPEC on other issues of direct Western self-interest? Former British chancellor of the exchequer, Denis Healey, saw the first building-blocks of Western-Arab cooperation in terms of fixed oil-price agreements:

> International economic diplomacy is like rowing a boat through treacle. I think the most hopeful area of agreement to aim at would probably involve the consumers' accepting regular small increases in price—at least indexed to inflation in the countries that provide OPEC with manufactured goods—in return for some guarantee of output from the producers. If we could create even one precedent for such cooperation between producers and consumers, wider agreements might flow from it. If we do not try, the situation is certain to deteriorate.[1]

It is now so difficult to negotiate directly with most members of OPEC—indeed, "negotiations" no longer occur—that the best development strategy may be to emphasize the plight of oil-importing Third World countries as the ground of common concern and to work progressively toward the issues where there now seems to be no starting point at all.

Certainly it seems that it would be easier to make progress on producer-consumer relations in an atmosphere lightened by success in other arenas. And even if most diplomatic negotiations fail to bear fruit, we would argue that three-cornered progress can still be made through quiet, unpublicized technical cooperation within Western and Arab aid programs, and among energy organizations like the IEA, OLADE, and others.

A second challenge is to ensure that new initiatives are not undermined by the mixture of motives that bring them into being. In an attempt to make sense of very large issues, we have discussed energy cooperation questions under five separate headings involving matters of foreign policy, technology, institutional programs, selected private investment, and policymaking in Third World countries. But it ought also to be clear that every energy decision faced by an aid donor will encounter some conflict between these viewpoints. For example, cooperating with OPEC donors on the development of renewable energy technologies seems sound enough from a foreign policy perspective. But so far, solar energy companies seem to believe that such cooperation would deny them some of the benefits of their investments to date by giving away trade secrets for diplomatic advantage, and they therefore remain sceptical.

Shifting combinations of special interests and conflicting motives have so far produced hybrid Third World energy policies in almost every aid-giving country. We would not argue that it is necessarily a bad thing that policies differ among aid donors, or even within different agencies of particular governments. But this situation does make for complicated selection and structuring of energy programs. The differences in approach between U.S. AID and the European Development Fund, both working in Mali, illustrated the international dimension of this problem (see Chapter 2). But its impact is more directly felt *within* aid-giving national governments, as they try to reconcile competing policy objectives. Certainly this is the case in the United States, where different government agencies are planning programs in the Third World that seem to share little in the way of common objectives.

The U.S. Department of Energy's plan to promote photovoltaic cells internationally, for example, ignores many of U.S. AID's objectives. DOE plans almost no effort to ensure that developmental and marketing objectives are matched to local circumstances in the purchasing countries. But is it really sensible to initiate a major U.S. international effort that ignores the issues of technology transfer that have plagued international aid and trade discussions for more than five years? The Department of Energy (or indeed any promotional mechanism in almost any Western country) would answer that the photovoltaic program is essentially designed to reduce the cost of solar energy, coincidentally selling American products, and that the program should not be judged by developmental or foreign policy standards. There is logic in this response, but it entirely begs the question of whether the U.S. government as a whole has decided what it can accomplish on energy cooperation with Third World countries, and how best to go about it.

One should not expect that any amount of careful thought or

planning can eliminate these kinds of conflicts among diverse interests. They are surely endemic to systems that mix governmental programs and private investment spurred by governmental incentives. But these conflicts could be better understood, and disparate programs reconciled, if the overriding objectives of energy policy toward the Third World were clarified and, where possible, agreed upon.

OLD INERTIA AND NEW IDEAS

It is still widely assumed in aid agencies and even in developing country governments that new energy solutions are a distant promise, still five or ten years over the horizon, but not a solution to today's problems. This assumption perhaps reflects the tendency of well-established biases to linger tenaciously, even when their economic justifications are collapsing. It is still difficult, for example, to locate many Third World energy specialists who pay much attention to the efficiency with which energy is used. They were trained simply to worry about increasing energy supplies.

The present dilemma is that while new energy sources appear to catch on and spread rapidly in use once they are boldly and widely introduced, they can only be introduced by development planners who have not until now grasped their advantages and are not therefore inclined to back them to the necessary degree. This is not to say that aid agency and government officials hold out any hope for the return of cheap conventional energy. They do not. But many of these officials remain unmoved by the myriad possibilities for energy conservation in agriculture and industry, for diversification of fossil fuel supplies, for replenishment of fuelwood stocks, and for a range of small but promising remote solar applications, which could all be acted on today. In short, concerted action has been impeded as much by a lag in planning and innovation as by any shortage of technical options.

On the other hand, blinkered idealism can equally frustrate its own objectives. Uncompromising efforts to achieve only the ideal arrangements and the perfect solutions can make it impossible to achieve quite modest steps forward. The time when reality conforms to the models of energy planners will never come. Developing countries are making new energy investment decisions every day (and falling further into debt). Time to formulate perfect programs is an unaffordable luxury because action is needed so urgently.

At both ends of the spectrum, the challenge is to break out of the inertia that has gripped energy planners and agencies. Despite many promising new initiatives, these institutions generally admit the inadequacy of measures taken to date. We will not at this stage attempt to recapitulate all of the positive steps that governments might take. Throughout this book we have indicated general directions and lines of approach. Here, our aim is to specify the type of major initiative that is needed: to assure adequate financing of aid programs, to adapt private investment in new energy sources to the circumstances of developing countries, and to achieve greater international cooperation on energy. Some of the needed actions can only be taken by governments, others could be initiated by aid programs or international institutions.

The Challenge to Governments

Proposals for increased development aid are not popular in the Western political climate of 1980. Efforts to locate and use new sources of energy have, however, an altogether better chance to capture the public imagination. Energy cooperation can help relieve the overall strain on global energy supplies and hasten the transition away from extreme fossil fuel dependence. The United States in particular among the Western aid donors can ill afford any further political isolation on energy, because its proportionate consumption of oil alienates both its Western allies and many of the Third World countries whose political stability is critical to world peace.

There is the danger that focusing funds on one aspect of development may imbalance development programs. Special funds or pledges are also sometimes resisted on the grounds that financial resources should not be mobilized until their dedication is carefully planned and committed. In the case of energy, it need hardly be said that the same logic was never applied to the development of nuclear power, which received vast subsidies in its developmental stages. But a better parallel is surely the commitment made by aid-giving nations in the sixties to transfer 1 percent of their GNPs to the developing world on concessional terms. Many nations, including the United States, fail year after year to keep this particular promise. But it stands as a solid reminder of the agreed level of effort that development assistance, as a whole, requires. In the same way, it is politically essential to begin now to subscribe funds on the scale that will be needed, three or five years from now, for strong and successful energy programs during the coming decade. Without major new financial pledges, new programs will tend to be designed solely to fit the level of support that is anticipated. In this era of increasing unpopularity of aid programs, that kind of planning may seem pragmatic but in fact tends to set off a self-limiting cycle of caution and inadequate funding. Worse, it leads to programs that may be "successful" by their own terms of reference, but that are wholly inadequate if measured by the scale of the problem they are meant to address.

At least three important activities are currently inadequately financed and should get priority attention. First, assured funding is needed for oil and gas development programs like the World Bank's, including the work of other institutions such as the UNDP.[a] Jointly financed projects with Arab aid agencies, some of which have already been agreed to, offer one important source of increased funding in this regard. International institutions in addition to the World Bank need supplementing money both to encourage oil and gas exploration and to provide an additional source of international "risk insurance." Second, widespread testing and demonstration projects are needed to encourage commercial development of new—particularly solar—technology. And finally, further concessional aid must be made available to create credit facilities for the purchase of small-scale renewable energy-using and energy-saving devices such as wood-burning stoves. (Without these greatly expanded credit operations, it will be difficult for poor energy *users* to become energy *purchasers.*)

We advocate the establishment of an international energy development fund, not as an autonomous new international organization but as a joint facility to receive payments by governments. Member governments' subscribing to the fund should ask the World Bank to establish it jointly with the reconstituted OPEC Fund, and the United Nations Development Programme.

The fund would not itself need the technical capacity to finance projects. It would provide loans on highly concessional terms, drawing upon the technical capabilities of the sponsoring institutions. Among other purposes, those loans could finance the payment of interest charges on ordinary development bank loans, for example those of the regional development banks. In the case of renewable energy technology projects, for example, this type of arrangement would enable the World Bank and the regional development banks to finance renewable energy projects sooner than would otherwise be

---

[a]It is particularly important that this type of program not be jeopardized by the uncertainties of donor (particularly American) appropriations. World Bank lending for oil/gas projects in middle-income countries would not be directly endangered by restraint in the aid appropriations process. The Bank loans to these countries are financed by the international sale of bonds, whose creditworthiness is underwritten by callable capital provided by donor governments. However, the poorest countries receive World Bank loans from the International Development Association (IDA) on highly concessional terms that cannot be underwritten by the international money market. IDA funds are replenished directly by governments. And the contributions of all other governments are tied by informal agreement to the U.S. contribution to IDA. If the U.S. replenishment of IDA is withheld, therefore, it affects *all* IDA funding and all projects.

the case (by supporting financially higher risk work on adaptation and application). The involvement of these institutions would, in turn, ensure that the development of renewable energy projects is not left exclusively in the hands of export-minded bilateral aid programs.

Apart from overcoming suspicion that an international energy fund would be a new guise for foreign aid, two complicated political issues would have to be resolved. First, Western resistance to special funding for energy often is based on the argument that Western governments should not raise money to counterbalance the effects on developing countries of OPEC price increases. That argument ignores the widespread Third World perception that oil price rises are caused by the intense bidding of Western consumers: That the cartel now follows the price rather than pushes it. More important to Western politicians, their resistance also ignores the direct benefits the West can expect from energy cooperation *regardless* of who "causes" oil price increases (see Chapter 1).

The second political hurdle poses more of a diplomatic challenge: Equitable fundraising among OECD countries would be difficult to accomplish. One approach might be for each OECD nation to contribute 1 percent of the value of its net petroleum imports. Under this formula, for instance, the U.S. contribution would be between $400–500 million annually. The difficulty with this system would be the burden it placed on countries like Japan and West Germany, heavily dependent on imported oil. The United States, as the dominant consumer, might become a disproportionately small contributor in the eyes of its allies. Another formula would tie payments to GNP, weighted by oil consumption and oil imports. This would obviously be more complicated, but leaves room for negotiation. The critical concern, which should never be allowed off center stage, is the need for the OECD countries to persuade OPEC nations to make a matching pledge. A high-visibility effort for the benefit of the developing countries who are most badly hurt by oil price increases would be difficult for OPEC to ignore. The return on this investment, through diversified world oil supply and a hastened transition to renewable energy sources, would be immense.

Firewood: The Top Priority

Of all the measures urgently needed in the poorest developing countries, firewood emerges as the first priority. Many of these countries face environmental and human catastrophe unless their exhaustion of firewood supplies is slowed and eventually reversed. It is surprising that only the American and Dutch aid agencies are so far ready to commit themselves to large firewood replenishment programs. The World Bank intends to incorporate wood plantation components in many of its forestry projects. But reforestation should also be a priority concern of very concessional bilateral aid, because the short-term economic return of afforestation projects makes them problematic for the conventional cost-benefit lending criteria of development banking institutions.

Development of oil and renewable energy resources is so clearly in direct Western self-interest that we have considered it separately from the firewood problem. Whether or not an international energy fund is launched to address those problems, we believe that every OECD bilateral aid program should commit itself in the Development Assistance Committee (DAC) of the OECD to participate in firewood projects and should confirm this commitment at the ministerial level of the OECD's Council. The Sahel has received considerable attention because of the work of the Committee on Interstate Drought Control in the Sahel and the Club du Sahel, and also due to the worldwide publicity generated by the famine of the early seventies, but other areas of the world are neglected. Agencies that lack sufficient forestry and agricultural staff could offer support through cofinancing with World Bank and regional development bank projects. The effort called for is daunting, and it is for this reason that we feel governmental leadership at the highest levels is essential.

Innovation in Technology Transfer

The third type of action that can only be expected to succeed if there is governmental support would perhaps be, eventually, the most far-reaching energy initiative that Northern countries could undertake. Private industrial investments in new sources of energy that are being attracted to Third World markets need not only to be stimulated, but also to be shaped innovatively. To transfer technology on terms more profitable politically and commercially than has been the case in other fields will require innovative consultation between buyers and sellers of the new energy technologies. The first steps can best be initiated under the leadership of the companies' home governments, particularly where those governments are using public funds to support the new energy industries, because the companies are clearly unlikely to cooperate on their own initiative. The vehicle might be a solar industry advisory service, for example, sponsored by a national government and consortium of industries within the OECD or the donor-coordinating mechanisms that are emerging.

This type of advisory group would aim to make a modest begin-

ning by encouraging an exchange of views among alternative energy
industries and Third World planners, researchers, and manufacturers.
These groups have rarely communicated with one another except on
a secretive, commercially competitive, individual basis. It should not
be excessively difficult, politically, to constitute such a group, because neither side has anything to lose by participating. Later on,
increasingly practical functions could be taken on. For example,
regional demonstration projects might be specified for competitive
bidding, or opportunities for joint ventures could be identified and
publicized.

At the outset, two types of participants should be involved. Representatives of a cross section of renewable energy industries (particularly the solar industry, given its export-mindedness) should
participate. If necessary, national industrial associations could be
asked to designate representatives. Third World representation
should particularly include government development planners but
should also embrace representatives of research facilities and private
industry. If narrowing of Third World representatives proved difficult, the developing country directors of the World Bank might
constitute themselves as an informal committee to make initial
suggestions.

Aid Programs and International Organizations

So far in this chapter, we have been discussing the large energy
issues, areas in which it seems certain that only governments can
take the lead. And we have argued that Western governments should
use these opportunities to identify new avenues of cooperation with
willing members of OPEC. But there are also a number of very important steps that aid programs, international development banks,
and U.N. agencies can take under the decision of their own leadership. Too much stress should not be laid here on formal coordination
among aid programs. Donors generally work quite closely together
on an informal basis, when the need is seen, and are unwilling to en-
gage in excessive, structured exchange of information and ideas.
Energy aid is changing rapidly, however, and for this reason, the informal consultative process started in June 1979 by the World Bank
should be put on a regular basis (see p. 75, above). The aim should
be to improve international cooperation on energy aid matters both
between bilateral and multilateral agencies on the one hand, and
between OPEC and Western aid funds on the other.

The World Bank's original interest was to explain and launch its
oil and gas program. Now donors need to set up an ad hoc working
group on energy assistance. It should emphatically not be designed

to allocate aid money among developing countries (a function that would meet bitter resistance), but should concentrate on technical cooperation and exchange. For example, one immediate objective of the group could be to sponsor methodological exchange on national energy assessments and to assure that as many countries as possible receive this type of assistance as soon as possible.

Donors should also seek agreement on more-open exchange of energy data gathered by project teams and missions (particularly including the great quantities of data generated for projects that failed to be approved). This goal relates closely to the creation of a forward planning mechanism so that agencies have advance warning of energy projects planned elsewhere and can allocate their own resources accordingly. In theory this already happens on an ad hoc basis, particularly among field staff, but in fact the existing system is grossly inefficient.

Finally, but most important, frameworks are needed in which to place new energy cooperation ventures that might otherwise flounder for lack of a fertile planting ground. For example, an energy working group of aid donors could be one logical setting for multilateral efforts to influence the directions taken by the solar energy industry. More formal channels might be needed, but it is almost certainly better to avoid the U.N. system, which is mistrusted by industry. Both industry and developing country governments and institutions would be most comfortable meeting on the neutral territory that a consortium of aid donors might provide.

The International Energy Agency should be encouraged by its member governments to continue to sponsor regular technical workshops, such as it held in December 1978. Indeed, a general enlargement of the IEA's "service" role would be a sure indicator to developing countries that the major industrialized powers are now serious about cooperation on energy matters, since the IEA's established responsibility has been exclusively to protect the most direct self-interest of its members. The IEA's official mandate need not be formally broadened, since technical cooperation is already one of its primary functions. But the agency staff is likely to be so overburdened by present oil supply conditions that its Governing Council should act to establish a small staff with permanent responsibility for technical cooperation with developing countries. Such a group should also have the expertise and authority to explore developing country participation in other mainstream IEA work. For example, the international energy technology group requested by the Tokyo summit might make a very significant contribution, linking renewable energy promoters and developing country users. Similarly, the

IEA could, without any revision in its procedures, enlarge its role as a center of North-South exchange on energy research programs.

Many of these activities, and others not mentioned here, will be debated at the August 1981 United Nations Conference on New and Renewable Sources of Energy, which was discussed in Chapter 3. It is impossible to evaluate the chances for a "successful" conference, but it ought to be recalled that the developing countries' definition of success will clearly differ from that of the OECD countries. The perception in the West of the United Nations system as an ineffective yet pretentious structure is not shared by developing countries, for whom it is important to their place in international diplomacy. Many Western countries may actually regard this latest United Nations conference as successful if it simply avoids blatant public failure. But these same governments accept the importance of emphasizing serious technical discussion, which is most likely to occur if there is already evidence of political progress elsewhere. In short, a United Nations conference is not a good place to launch new ideas, but it is the inevitable forum for gathering support behind them.

Action Today: Practical Measures

The large portrait of improved financing and major political initiative is likely to remain clouded for a long time. But even while new energy debates occur, aid agencies and institutions should press forward with practical changes in policy and programs. We have spoken of the need for a great deal more planning assistance, training, and institutional strengthening in developing country energy departments to enable them to determine their own energy strategies. In fact, a major new effort behind this type of energy aid could be the vital link between diplomatic initiative and practical action. This type of help is necessary for two reasons. First, developing countries have little reason to take energy advice from the great energy consumers and many reasons to suspect it. So the new technologies and the new sources of energy that the North will be promoting are more likely to prove acceptable if understood and planned for by the poor countries themselves. Donor countries will also find this approach advantageous in that it will help to protect them from blame and resentment that may arise when investments fail or experiments go awry. There will be mistakes—in North and South—as new energy programs are sifted and implemented. Aid donors will not want to be fully responsible for those that occur in the South.

National energy assessments are needed immediately where these have not been conducted. The urgency of the need for them arises from the fact that energy investment decisions are being made every day. Alternative approaches and procedures need to be tested, and a major effort is needed to enlarge their credibility in the eyes of host governments, perhaps by financing multidonor assessments. National assessments should include significant participation by nationals of the host country and should always be backed by training programs geared to establishing an energy planning capability in the host country.

A second step for aid programs is a much larger concentration of effort to train developing country energy experts at every level of sophistication. Some training work can be done in Europe or North America. For example, the French government brings Third World nationals to petroleum development programs in France, and U.S. AID sponsors a six-week course at the Brookhaven National Laboratory to develop skills needed for energy development and management. But a great deal more training is also needed in the developing countries to prepare maintenance and installation technicians (both for the introduction of new energy technologies and for better up-keep and utilization of existing or traditional systems). In particular, to build up the indigenous capability of those developing country institutions that have energy responsibilities, aid programs should seek out experts in national scientific research institutions, help them upgrade their knowledge, and encourage their involvement in the various stages of project development. This will help raise the standing of these scientists with their governments and also help them acquire the confidence and experience needed to share the task of energy planning and project implementation with development aid institutions.

It has become almost commonplace to suggest that more research is needed on developing country energy needs and resources. While this is true, we would emphasize the great need for concentrating research efforts in a few key areas whose neglect has the potential to cause serious misdirection of investment. The full costs and benefits of choices among energy systems (marginal investments in centralized versus decentralized and renewable versus nonrenewable electrification, and electrification versus primary energy applications in any particular setting) have, so far as can be ascertained, remained largely uncompared. The World Bank has apparently reevaluated the economics of central station rural electrification. This research should be shared with other donors and made public. Likewise, hydroelectric power projects seem to be enjoying a resurgence, and there appears to be a widespread renewal of interest in large dams as part of major regional development schemes. It is essential here to ensure that many of the flagrant mistakes of the past are not repeated.

Joint research efforts between developing country researchers and Northern institutions (aid programs *and* technical or energy ministries) are also an important new initiative. Too often, developing country research institutions lack adequate facilities and staff and cannot find sufficient support in their own governments. Increased aid agency support for, and cooperation with, these institutions may catalyze national efforts. Donor involvement may also reduce the incidence of "pure" research that is essentially wasted by being swamped by parallel efforts elsewhere. Applied research—the type of work that can only be done well on a local basis—should receive the highest priority support of aid programs.

A different type of aid agency involvement is needed to finance "low technology" energy projects such as biogas digesters, windmills made of local materials, and small nonturbine hydroelectric generators. These projects have low foreign-exchange requirements and limited technology transfer components. Many badly needed energy projects—biogas, for example—require almost *no* foreign-exchange component and *no* transfer of Northern technology. To facilitate financing of this type of project as well as to encourage the adaptation of solar and other technologies, several innovations are badly needed.

There are at least three opportunities for aid agencies to increase their prospects for financing very small energy projects on a local scale. First, the authority of local aid officers to authorize small loans and grants should be increased. Regulations in this area are ordinarily excessively complex, but despite significant bureaucratic barriers, this could be one area of significant, quick change. Second, industrial development banks and national development banks in the developing countries could be mobilized for these purposes. These institutions can make small loans at very concessional interest rates, and this could be done on a sectoral basis. Naturally, Third World governments prefer funds that are not earmarked for a sector, but loans could be advanced for institutions that indicate an interest in the energy area. It seems clear that a special effort is needed to cut red tape and make funds available to local manufacturers and users of the new energy technologies. Third, multilateral agencies should try to establish better links with private voluntary organizations. This has for some time been seen as a critical area for encouraging new initiatives with alternative energy, because these small groups almost always work with local populace in developing countries and so have a unique position from which to advise on the social and cultural problems that new energy systems are likely to encounter. Grants to these agencies for project purposes are ordinarily quite small, but all of the major bilateral agencies have funds for this type of activity. (The World Bank and most regional development banks have not.)

BEYOND STALEMATE?

This book is written at a time when hopes for progress in its two main areas of concern, energy and development, seem dim if not forbidding. Development assistance is politically unpopular in the West, both because it lacks powerful domestic constituencies and because we face a time of economic retrenchment. Economic "independence" seems to be gaining popularity as a political banner just as economic interdependence becomes increasingly unavoidable. Energy policies encompass problems of a different character, due to their entanglement with intense domestic politics in every Western country. It seems certain that the energy crisis of the West will tax our human and financial resources for years to come.

Those who believe that today's policies toward the Third World should simply be tougher, boiled down versions of yesterday's are not looking carefully at the world about them. To begin with, control of the world's capital resources has shifted dramatically. It is more dispersed than ever before. And the developing nations themselves, after learning that "development" does not automatically follow the drafting of successive five-year plans, are politically and economically more volatile than at any time since independence. Their instability cannot be confined to the southern continents; it shows every sign of affecting Western interests in immeasurable ways in the coming decade.

Against all of this, we have put forward some rather modest suggestions for working toward one idea: that it is possible to cooperate with the less developed countries and the members of OPEC, working together to improve the energy position of all. We have argued that new institutional creations are not likely to break existing logjams, but would only complicate them. The cumulative effect of the measures proposed here would, of course, not alone solve any of the Third World's energy problems. Our hope was not to set forth specific solutions in great detail, but to contribute to a changing climate in which new types of measures are considered and negotiated.

Failure to take decisive action now and at every future opportunity will turn a worsening situation into a virtually hopeless one in some parts of the world, and help to aggravate political confrontations regionally, and perhaps internationally, at incalculable cost. The development plans of many Third World nations—along with their belief that a better life is possible—hang in the balance. So, too, do hopes for a new energy order based on anything other than the starkest political and perhaps military confrontation. The energy problems of the Third World are at least as challenging as those faced by the industrialized countries, which, it seems, have only one sensible choice: to join with far greater effort in the search for practical solutions.

NOTES

1. Denis Healey, "Oil, Money and Recession" *Foreign Affairs* 58, 2 (Winter 1979/80), p. 226. Reprinted by permission from *Foreign Affairs* (Winter 1979/80); Copyright 1979 by Council on Foreign Relations, Inc.

✳ Appendix 1

The Venezuelan Investment Fund

Organized in June 1974, the Venezuelan Investment Fund (VIF) began operations in April 1975. The fund's initial resources were approximately 3.1 billion dollars and, beginning in 1975, resources were automatically increased by means of annual appropriations amounting to 50 percent of all fiscal revenues arising from petroleum and gas taxes applied to the same activities. It appears that at the end of 1975, VIF resources equaled 5 billion dollars.

VIF's charter prohibits grants, and the VIF also cannot make direct loans to foreign governments, except in the case of lending operations carried out through trust funds established by the VIF in official international institutions. The largest such fund is administered by the Inter-American Development Bank.

By 1975 the VIF had completed agreements with ten institutions: the Inter-American Development Bank, the Andean Development Corporation, the Caribbean Development Bank, the Central America Bank for Economic Integration, the National Bank of Panama, and the central banks of five Central American states.

An UNCTAD report describes the bilateral agreements between the VIF and the five Central American banks and the National Bank of Panama as follows:

The general objectives are twofold: to mitigate the short-run impact of higher import costs of Venezuelan petroleum on the balance of payments of the recipient countries, and to finance longer term programmes and projects designed to develop their natural resources and to promote the diversification of their exports. In order to achieve the first of these objectives, the VIF reimburses, through six-year time deposits (half in dollars and half in bolivars), the difference between a "basic price" of six dollars per barrel and the actual market prices of Venezuelan petroleum imported by the recipient countries. [This arrangement has been limited to set volumes of petroleum] . . . which decrease by one-sixth each successive year until the arrangement expires at the end of 1980.[a] However, the deposits may be converted into twenty-five-year loans or investments for programmes and projects covered by the second objective.

. . . The bilateral arrangements between the VIF and the central banking institutions of Central America and Panama envisage a different kind of financial technique. In the first stage, i.e., the medium-term balance of payments support, the typical operation takes the form of deposits at the Central Bank of Venezuela (denominated in dollars and Venezuelan bolivars) in favor of the recipient central banks. These deposits are made quarterly after the actual price paid by the recipient countries for petroleum imports from Venezuela has been determined. *In the second stage, such deposits may be reimbursed in exchange for longer-term loans or equity participations designed to meet the local currency requirements of development programmes or projects already being financed by the World Bank, IDB, or CABEI* [emphasis added]. The deposits may also be converted into longer-term loans designed to finance export credit programmes, in accordance with the policy criteria and limitations provided for in the trust agreement between the VIF and the IDB.

. . . In the special case of the bilateral arrangements between the VIF and the central banking institutions of Central America and Panama, maturities vary according to the purpose of the financing operation, (i.e., up to six years for balance of payments purposes and up to twenty-five years for development projects), but all interest charges are linked to the rate applied by IDB in its ordinary loan operations, which is currently fixed at 8 percent per annum. Although for the time being the VIF allows recipient banks freely to invest the proceeds of the time deposits in the international money markets, the cost of first-stage operations could not always be fully offset during the first half of 1975.

. . . The time deposits made by the VIF in the central banking institutions of Central America and Panama are being denominated—and must

[a]In 1975 this was (volumes in barrels per day):

Costa Rica	7,300
Honduras	14,800
El Salvador	11,400
Nicaragua	8,900
Guatemala	14,800
Panama	13,600

Source: United Nations, Conference on Trade and Development, *Financial Solidarity for Development—Efforts and Institutions of the Members of OPEC,* TD/B/627, New York: United Nations, 1977. Reprinted with permission of UNCTAD.

be reimbursed—in equal parts in dollars and bolivars. However, if such deposits are converted into longer term development loans, the latter must be denominated and repaid in bolivars only. This obviously means that the recipient central banks, governments, or private enterprises must bear any exchange risks arising from a revaluation of the Venezuelan currency, thus increasing the financial cost of borrowing from the VIF.

✳ Appendix 2

Saudi Arabian/U.S. Solar Cooperation Agreement (SOLERAS I)

On October 30, 1977, representatives of the U.S. Department of Energy and Department of Treasury, jointly, and the Saudi Arabian National Center for Science and Technology and the Saudi Arabian Ministry of Finance and National Energy, jointly, signed a five-year agreement for "Cooperation in the Field of Solar Energy." SOLERAS I (Solar Energy Research American Saudi) aims to increase "cooperation in solar technology development and to facilitate the transfer of solar technology." The $100 million, five-year project is funded equally by the United States and Saudi Arabia and theoretically includes all types of solar systems and technologies (centralized and dispersed solar thermal, photovoltaics, biomass, wind, and ocean). The scope of the project is large and includes joint research, development, and demonstration projects; exchange visits by specialist teams of individuals; and educational exchange opportunities for training or study.

As part of this comprehensive agreement, two Saudi Arabian villages will be equipped with 350 kilowatts of photovoltaic cells and a supporting electrical system (transmission equipment, storage equipment, and loads). In September 1979, the $16.5 million contract to design, build, install, and maintain this solar energy project was awarded to the Martin Marietta Corporation of Bethesda, Maryland, a leading U.S. aerospace contractor.

The 350-kw system will provide all of the power needs of Al Jubailah and part of those of Al Uyaynah, neighboring villages approximately thirty miles northwest of the capital city of Riyadh. A photovoltaic system using concentrating and tracking devices to produce 50 kw peak power will be installed in July 1980, and another 300 kw will be added by March 1981. Uses being considered for this output are lighting, refrigeration, air-conditioning, telecommunications, irrigation pumping, and water desalinization. As part of this program, an extensive effort will be made to document the impact of the introduction of this technology on the local villagers, its acceptance or rejection and a wide variety of other sociological observations.

As project planning under the SOLERAS agreement has proceeded, some observers have questioned whether such a program will help the Saudis to develop an independent solar capability or whether it will simply boost exports of U.S. solar equipment. For example, although bidding for the 350-kw project was open to both U.S. and Saudi firms, very few Saudi firms actually responded. Of course, this is a result of the small amount of solar research work being done in Saudi Arabian solar firms, and the fact that most of the companies that exist are offshoots or extensions of U.S. firms. Even though at present some solar work is being done at four or five Saudi research institutions and a couple of major universities in the country, its contribution to the SOLERAS projects has been very limited indeed when compared to U.S. participation.

Sources: Wendy Peters, "Photovoltaic Cells to Generate Villages' Power under Saudi/U.S. Agreement," *Canadian Renewable Energy News*, May 1979.
Wall Street Journal, September 27, 1979.
Anil Agarwal, *Whose Solar Power?* Earthscan Press-Briefing Document No. 19 (London: Earthscan Press, 1979).
DOE Solar Energy Domestic Policy Review International Panel, Technical Cooperation Sub Report, "Review and Assessment of DOE Technical Cooperation Agreements" (U.S. Department of Energy, August 22, 1978).

✳ Appendix 3

Scope for Petroleum Exploration in Developing Countries

The survey commissioned by the World Bank on the oil and gas situation in seventy developing countries provides the best available information on the size of prospective petroleum areas, onshore and offshore, past seismic and exploratory drilling activities, the existing permit and contract situation, and the outlook for exploration in the near term. Twenty-three countries have prospects of finding "high" or "very high" quantities of petroleum, while a further fifteen have prospects of locating "fair" quantities as defined below.

Table 1: Petroleum Prospects of Seventy Developing Countries

Type of Country	No. of Countries	Size of Potential Resources			
		Very High	High	Fair	Low
Oil producer/net importer	12	6	3	2	1
Nonproducer/known reserves	10	4	2	3	1
Nonproducer/no discoveries	45	1	4	10	30
Non-OPEC producer/exporter	3	2	1	0	0
Total	70	13	10	15	32

Note: Potential resources are classified into four main categories on the basis of estimated recoverable quantities: *Very High*—over 1,500 m. barrels; *High*—between 750 and 1,500 m.; *Fair*—between 100 and 750 m.; *Low*—less than 100 m. barrels. Measured by the reserves of OPEC countries, even the "Very High" category is modest. But in terms of domestic consumption, the "Low" category may be very significant . . . .

Exploration statistics must be interpreted with caution, and there is no consensus among governments or in the oil industry on how much activity is adequate. What may appear appropriate from a global point of view may be wholly insufficient from the viewpoint of an oil-importing LDC with reasonable prospects of finding or enlarging reserves of petroleum. Using the criterion that an adequate level of exploration is one that is likely to lead to the early identification of exploitable reserves, the study prepared for the World Bank classified the seventy developing countries as shown in Table 5:

Table 2: Adequacy of Exploration in Seventy Developing Countries

Type of Country	No. of Countries	Exploration Activities		
		Inadequate	Moderate	Adequate
Oil producer/net importer	12	6	4	2
Nonproducer/known reserves	10	3	3	4
Nonproducer/no discoveries	45	28	13	4
Non-OPEC producer/exporter	3	1	2	0
Total	70	38	22	10

Note: If the above findings are compared to those on petroleum prospects (Table 4), it appears that only seven of the twenty-three countries with high or very high prospects have been explored adequately; six have been explored moderately and the rest inadequately. Of the fifteen countries with fair prospects, only one has been explored adequately, and the rest moderately (three) or inadequately (eleven).

Reproduced by permission, from *A Program to Accelerate Petroelum Production in the Developing Countries* (Washington D.C.: World Bank, January 1979).

 **Appendix 4**

Statistical Tables

Table 1. Energy Position of Developing Countries by Levels of Energy Consumption, Import Dependence, and Reserves

Per Capita Commercial Energy Consumption (1975)
(in kilograms of coal equivalent)

Net Imports of Energy as a Percentage of Total Commercial Energy Consumption	Less than 200 — Group I				200–1000 — Group II				More than 1,000 — Group III			
	Country	SF	ONG	HY	Country	SF	ONG	HY	Country	SF	ONG	HY
Less than 25%	Afghanistan[a]		x	x	Algeria[a]		x	x	Argentina		x	x
	Angola[a]		x	x	Bolivia[a]		x	x	Bahrain[a]		x	
	Burma		x	x	Colombia[a]	x	x	x	Brunei[a]		x	
	Indonesia[a]	x	x	x	Congo[a]		x	x	Gabon[a]		x	x
	Nigeria	x	x	x	Ecuador[a]		x	x	Iran[a]	x	x	x
					Egypt	x	x	x	Israel	x		
					India	x	x	x	Kuwait[a]		x	
					Iraq[a]		x	x	Libya[a]		x	
					Malaysia		x		Mexico[a]	x	x	x
					Oman[a]		x		Qatar[a]		x	
					Syria[a]		x		Saudi Arabia[a]		x	x
					Tunisia[a]		x		Trinidad and Tobago		x	
									United Arab Emirates[a]		x	
									Venezuela[a]	x	x	x

25% to 75%

	Group IV		Group V		Group VI	
Mozambique	x		Brazil	x	Rep. of Korea	x x
Pakistan	x x		Chile	x x		
Rwanda		x	Peru	x		
			Zambia	x x		

More than 75%

	Group VII		Group VIII		Group IX	
Bangladesh	x	Costa Rica	x	x	Barbados	x
Benin	x	Dominican Republic	x		Cyprus	
Burundi		El Salvador		x	Guyana	x
Central African Empire		Fiji			Jamaica	
United Republic of Cameroon	x	Guadaloupe		x	Malta	x
Chad	x	Guatemala		x	Singapore	x
Ethiopia	x	Honduras	x	x	Surinam	x
Gambia	x	Ivory Coast				
Ghana	x	Jordan				
Guinea	x	Lebanon		x		
Guinea-Bissau	x	Liberia		x		
Haiti		Mauritius				
Kenya	x	Morocco	x	x		
Madagascar	x	Nicaragua		x		
Malawi		Panama				
Mali	x	Papua New Guinea	x			
Mauritania	x	Philippines	x	x		
Nepal		Thailand	x	x		
Niger	x	Uruguay		x		
Paraguay	x					
Senegal	x	Tanzania	x	x		

continued

Table 1.   continued

Net Imports of Energy as a Percentage of Total Commercial Energy Consumption	Per Capita Commercial Energy Consumption (1975) (in kilograms of coal equivalent)											
	Less than 200				200–1000				More than 1,000			
	Country[a]	Reserves			Country	Reserves			Country	Reserves		
		SF	ONG	HY		SF	ONG	HY		SF	ONG	HY
	Sierra Leone			x								
	Somalia			x								
	Sri Lanka			x								
	Sudan			x								
	Tanzania		x									
	Togo											
	Uganda			x								
	Upper Volta			x								
	Yemen			x								
	Zaire	x	x									

SOURCE: This is an amended, simplified version of Table 6, Energy Position of Developing Countries and Territories by Levels of Energy Consumption. Import Dependence and Reserves, in *Energy Supplies for Developing Countries: Issues in Transfer and Development of Technology. A Study by the UNCTAD Secretariat*, Ref. B/C. 6/31, October 1978. Reproduced with permission from the *Report of the OECD Working Party of the Council to Develop a Co-ordinated Effort to Help Developing Countries Bring into Use Technologies Related to Renewable Energy.*

NOTES: SF = Solid Fuels
ONG = Oil and Natural Gas
HY = Hydro resources

Marking of an "x" for a given resource against a given country signifies:

(i)   50 million metric tons of coal equivalent of proved reserves for solid fuels;
(ii) 100 million barrels of proved reserves for oil and 1,000 billion cubic feet of proved reserves for natural gas;
(iii) 1,000 MW of installed and installable hydroelectric potential based on the average historical annual flow.

a Implies net exporters of energy.

Table 2. Summary of R and D Activities in Nonconventional Sources of Energy in Developing Countries

Country	Solar heating	Solar cooling of building	Crop drying	Water pumping	Solar electricity: thermal	Solar electricity: photovoltaic	Wind energy	Biological energy	Energy from the sea	Geothermal energy
Argentina	x		x			x	x			
Barbados			x				x			
Bolivia			x			x	x			
Brazil	x		x			x				
Chad		x			x		x			
Chile	x				x					x
China	x		x							
Costa Rica	x		x				x			
Cuba		x					x			
Ecuador	x									
Egypt	x			x	x		x			
El Salvador										x
Guatemala	x		x							
India	x			x	x	x	x			
Iran	x		x		x	x				
Iraq	x									
Israel	x	x		x	x	x		x		
Jamaica	x		x							
Jordan	x									
Kuwait	x				x	x				
Malawi	x		x							
Malaysia		x	x		x	x		x		
Mali		x			x					
Mauritius			x							
Niger				x	x	x				
Nigeria			x							
Oman					x		x			
Pakistan	x	x	x			x		x		
Papua New Guinea			x	x						
Peru	x		x							
Phlippines	x		x				x			x
Qatar					x					
Saudi Arabia	x		x	x	x	x				
Senegal	x				x					
Singapore					x			x		
Sri Lanka	x		x	x			x			
Sudan			x							
Thailand			x	x			x			
No. of countries engaged	22	7	21	8	15	10	12	4	—	3
No. of countries listed	58	18	55	21	39	26	32	11	—	8

SOURCE: United Nations, "Research in nonconventional sources of energy: Report of the Secretary-General" January 1979, Annex (Summary of responses sent by the Member States of the UN to the Sec.-General's verbal note concerning their current programs in research and development in nonconventional sources of energy).

NOTE: Reproduced by permission of UNCTAD, from "Energy Supplies for Developing Countries: Issues in Transfer and Development of Technology," a study prepared in October 1978 by the UNCTAD secretariat.

Table 3. Comparison of Current Annual Rural Afforestation Programs in Selected Developing Countries with the Approximate Size of Program Needed to Meet Domestic Fuelwood Requirements to the Year 2000

Country	Current Annual Fuelwood Afforestation Program	Approximate Annual Program Needed to Meet Domestic Fuelwood Requirements to the Year 2000	Total Planting Target Needed by the Year 2000 to Meet Domestic Requirements	Factor Indicating by How Much the Present Annual Rate of Planting Would Have to Be Increased to Meet Domestic Requirements to the Year 2000
	(000's of ha)	(000's of ha)[a]	(million ha)	
Rwanda	1.5	13.0	0.26	8.6
Burundi	1.5	5.4	0.11	3.6
Malawi	2.5	13.0	0.26	5.2
Tanzania	2.5	20.0	0.40	8.0
Sierra Leone	0.5	2.5	0.05	5.0
Niger	0.5	3.5	0.07	7.0
Mali	0.5	4.0	0.08	8.0
Nigeria	10.0	100.0	2.00	10.0
Ethiopia	1.0	50.0	1.00	50.0
Nepal	5.0	50.0	1.00	10.0
Thailand	10.0	75.0	1.50	7.5
India	20.0	250.0	5.00	12.5
Afghanistan	1.0	50.0	1.00	50.0
Peru	5.0	20.0	0.40	4.0
Ecuador	2.0	13.0	0.26	6.5
Totals	63.5	669.4	13.39	.....

SOURCE: World Bank data, 1978. Table compiled by John S. Spears, Forestry Advisor, World Bank, Washington, D.C. Included as table in paper presented at the 103d Annual Meeting of the American Forestry Association, October 8, 1978, entitled "Wood as an Energy Source: The Situation in the Developing World." Reprinted with permission.

[a] Based on the assumption that between one-third and one-half of total rural energy requirements could be met by other forms of energy than wood, such as biogas plants or solar cookers and by introducing greater end-use efficiency.

Table 4.   International Energy Aid by Major Multilateral and Bilateral Donors

This series of tables indicates the energy aid activity for the periods as given for each of the following agencies and countries:

Multilateral Aid

World Bank

Asian Development Bank

Inter-American Development Bank

OPEC Fund

United Nations Development Programme

United Nations Centre for Natural Resources, Energy and Transport

European Development Fund

Bilateral Aid

Canada

France

Federal Republic of Germany

Kuwait

Netherlands

United Kingdom

United States

It was impossible to obtain energy aid data for comparable periods for all agencies, primarily because the agencies themselves maintain statistical records with widely differing systems. Therefore, specific comparisons of size of programs should be made with caution. With the exception of three programs (the bilateral aid programs of the Federal Republic of Germany and the Netherlands, and the European Development Fund), however, general comparisons of order of magnitude may safely be made.

WORLD BANK

Financing for energy projects has historically accounted for one-fifth of World Bank lending. Between FY 1972 and FY 1978, the International Bank for Reconstruction and Development lent $5.59 billion for energy projects.

The Bank's activities in the energy field have been concentrated primarily in electric power projects, although loans representing $750 million have been approved for nineteen oil and gas related projects through FY 1978. Fourteen of these loans were directed toward pipeline infrastructure, four projects concerned coal development, and one project related to oil and gas development.

In July 1977 the Bank decided to finance oil and natural gas production during the early 1980s, and in January 1979 this program was increased, and also enlarged to include exploration projects. The Bank approved a $150 million loan to India in 1977 for developing its Bombay High offshore field. In FY 1979, the World Bank (including the International Finance Corporation) approved $106.5 million in loans for oil and gas development in five countries. In FY 1980, another sixteen loans are planned, totaling approximately $490.4 million. A further $30.8 million in loans are planned for oil and gas exploration in 1980. The Bank also will increase loans for coal exploration and recovery.

In the area of new and renewable resources, the World Bank has funded some small biomass components of larger projects, and is currently executing a UNDP demonstration project for solar pumps in India, Sudan, Mali, and the Philippines. In addition, the Bank is beginning to include stove construction components in some of its forestry projects.

The World Bank has recently begun lending for geothermal projects (El Salvador, Kenya, and Honduras) and is also initiating a large number of energy sector studies through 1981.

Table 4A.1.   World Bank (FY 1972–December 1978)

Type of Project	No. of Projects	Amount ($US Millions)	% of Total Energy Lending
Power generation			
Hydroelectric	28	1,490.4	26.20
Thermal	38	1,479.5	26.00
Subtotal	66	2,969.9	52.20
Transmission and distribution			
Rural electrification	7	252.0	4.40
Other	38	1,988.5	35.00
Fossil fuels recovery	4	305.4	5.40
Nuclear energy	0	0.0	0.00
Renewable energy[a]	2	1.2	0.02
Fuelwood[b]	22	93.8	1.60
Geothermal energy	3	75.3	1.30
Total	142	5,686.1	100.00

SOURCE: Annual Reports FY 1972–Dec. 1978.

[a]The Ulla Ulla Rural Development Project was approved early in 1978 for a total of $18 million. It includes $120,000 for Bolivian research on solar cookers. A 1975 loan to Israel involves research on solar ponds and five "prime movers" (engines), which are being designed for use with a variety of nonconventional energy sources. These two components accounted for $1.1 million of a $35 million loan.

[b]Projects in the category "Fuelwood" are frequently, in fact, fuelwood plantation components of projects in other sectors.

Table 4A.2. World Bank Loans and IDA Credits to Electric Power Sector
(FY 1972–FY 1978)

Year	Amount ($US Millions)	Total Bank Lending for Year ($US Millions)	% Total Lending
1972	520.6	2,965.9	18
1973	321.5	3,407.7	9
1974	769.4	4,313.6	18
1975	503.7	5,895.8	9
1976	949.3	6,632.4	14
1977	951.5	7,066.8	13
1978	1,146.2	8,410.7	14

SOURCE: Annual Reports FY 1972–FY 1978.

ASIAN DEVELOPMENT BANK

From 1972 through the end of 1978, the ADB committed over $1,182 million in loans to the electric power sector, approximately 23 percent of total ADB lending and the largest commitment to any single sector. The Bank's operations give priority to (1) indigenous resource-based generation, primarily hydropower; (2) rehabilitation and repair of existing generation facilities; and (3) reduction of system losses. The Bank so far has only financed rural electrification as part of larger distribution projects. The ADB also provides funds for expertise in planning and operating power plants.

The Bank plans to extend assistance for development of institutional capability to carry out geological and geophysical surveys in order to enable member countries to locate possible resources of fuels and other minerals. The assistance will consist mainly of training for local staff, as well as provision of equipment and facilities for carrying out the surveys. Although the Bank has so far not granted loans for oil exploration, a loan for natural gas development in Bangladesh is planned for 1980. Loans for coal development have been extended to Korea and the Philippines, and a coal gasification plant loan in Pakistan is planned for 1981.

In addition the ADB is currently assisting Thailand ($250,000) to carry out an energy sector master plan.

The Bank expresses an interest in geothermal, wind, solar, and biogas energy sources, but so far has not funded projects in these areas. It has, however, recently begun to include fuelwood components in some forestry projects.

Table 4B.1.   Asian Development Bank (FY 1971-FY 1978)

Type of Project	No. of Projects	Amount ($US Millions)	% of Total Energy Lending
Power generation			
Hydroelectric	21	395.6	32.9
Thermal	22	227.2	18.9
Other	4	82.7	6.9
Subtotal	47	705.5	58.6
Transmission and Distribution	31	477.4	39.7
Fossil fuels recovery	2	20.8	1.7
Nuclear energy	0	0	0
Renewable energy	0	0	0
Geothermal energy	0	0	0
Total	80	1,203.7	100.0

SOURCE: Annual Reports FY 1972-FY 1978.

Table 4B.2.   ADB Loans to Electric Power Sector (FY 1972-FY 1978)

Year	No. of Projects	Amount ($US Millions)	Total Bank Lending for Year ($US Millions)	% Total Lending
1972	11	121.1	316.1	38
1973	11	92.5	421.5	22
1974	4	76.5	547.7	14
1975	10	139.9	660.3	21
1976	3	128.7	775.9	17
1977	9	217.6	887.0	25
1978	7	249.2	1,158.7	22

SOURCE: Annual Reports FY 1972-FY 1978.

NOTE: In addition:
1974—(1) Technical assistance for Bangladesh Energy Study, total cost $1.3 million (included survey of rural energy needs).
(2) Sui Karachi Gas Pipeline Project in Pakistan, total cost $53.17 million.
1975—Greater Dacca Gas Distribution Project in Bangladesh, total cost $12.20 million.
1976—Coal development loan in South Korea, total cost $12 million.
1978—Mineral resource development in South Korea, $8.0 million.
1978—OPEC-funded, ADB-executed:
(1) Pakistan, Tarbela hydro—$13.0 million.
(2) Sri Lanka, Bowakana power—$3.15 million.

INTER-AMERICAN DEVELOPMENT BANK

The energy sector has traditionally taken 25 percent of the IDB's annual portfolio. The IDB has given approximately $2.76 billion in loans to the energy sector from FY 1972 to FY 1978, with heavy emphasis on large hydroelectric projects and improved transmission and distribution systems. Recently the Bank financed a coal-mining project for a thermal electric plant. In addition, the IDB is considering financing an investigation of solar energy potential in the Dominican Republic.

In the area of technical cooperation, the Bank has supported projects designed to strengthen energy-related institutions, financed prefeasibility, feasibility, and final-design studies, and preparation of long-range electric generation plants. It has financed electric power subsector studies in several countries. Within a broader context, the IDB has approved an initial technical cooperation grant for a study in the Dominican Republic to identify opportunities to increase efficient energy use in industry and transportation.

The IDB is considering financing two studies to quantify gas and petroleum reserves. In addition, geological studies for oil and gas in Barbados, amounting tentatively to $1.5 million, are being considered. In Costa Rica, the Bank is supporting a feasibility study to determine geothermal potential, which could lead to a further loan for electricity generation.

According to a recent decision by the board of governors, approximately 25 percent of total lending in the 1979–1982 period, or $2 billion, is to be allocated to the energy sector, including the development and utilization of both conventional and nonconventional energy resources. The Bank is also contemplating the establishment of a special insurance and guarantee fund for the development of regional energy and mineral resources, including both fuel and nonfuel minerals.

Table 4C.1.   Inter-American Development Bank (FY 1972–FY 1978)

Type of Project	No. of Projects	Amount ($US Millions)	% of Total Energy Lending
Power generation			
Hydroelectric	24	1,681.1	60.9
Thermal	0	0	—
Subtotal	24	1,681.1	60.9
Transmission and Distribution			
Rural Electrification	8	181.5	6.6
Other	15	733.5	26.6
Fossil fuels recovery	1	158.0	5.7
Nuclear energy	0	0	0
Renewable energy[a]	0	0	0
Geothermal energy	1	4.1	0.2
Total	49	2,758.2	100.0

SOURCE: Annual Reports FY 1972–FY 1978.

[a] In 1978, the IDB provided short-term technical cooperation missions amounting to $1.09 million to the Dominican Republic for preparation and studies leading to an increase in efficiency of energy use and for an applied investigation program in use of solar energy technology, especially in the rural areas.

Table 4C.2.   IDB Loans to Electric Power Sector (FY 1972–FY 1978)

Year	No. of Projects	Amount ($US Millions)	Total Bank Lending for Year ($US Millions)	% Total Lending
1972	6	233.0	807	29
1973	5	216.0	884	24
1974	7	384.0	1,111	35
1975	6	304.0	1,375	22
1976	7	214.0	1,528	14
1977	8	391.1	1,809	22
1978	9	764.8	1,870	41

SOURCE: Annual Reports, FY 1972–FY 1978.

NOTE: In addition:

1972—Uruguay: Offshore petroleum terminal, loan $10.0 million.

1973—Bolivia: Expansion of oil refinery, loan $46.5 million.

1976—Argentina: Gas pipeline project, loan $87.0 million.
      Ecuador: Oil and gas pipeline project, loan $36.0 million.

1977—Argentina: Gas pipeline project expansion, loan $36.0 million.

1978—Mexico: Coal mining, loan $158.0 million.

OPEC FUND

THE OPEC Fund was established in 1976 as a collective development aid fund of the thirteen member countries of OPEC. Initially endowed with $800 million, the Fund's total resources have more than doubled, and a further replenishment of 1.6 billion was announced in 1979.

The OPEC Fund maintains an extremely small staff and therefore relies almost exclusively (in the energy field and in all other sectors) on opportunities for cofinancing projects with other aid institutions.

The Fund's largest single activity so far has been its contribution of $435.5 million to the International Fund for Agricultural Development (IFAD). The OPEC Fund makes balance-of-payments support loans, as well as loans for development projects. In the field of energy, as the following table illustrates, the Fund has largely concentrated in electric power generation and distribution, although it has, through the UNDP, begun to participate in comprehensive energy planning (initially through a project in Central America). Hydropower has been emphasized, so far receiving over $60 million in loans and balance of payments support.

Table 4D.   OPEC Fund (1977-present)

Type of Project	No. of Projects	Amount ($US Millions)	% of Total Energy Financing
Hydroelectric power	22	65.329	35.1
Thermal power	9	66.100	35.6
Power distribution	4	36.950	19.9
Fossil fuels recovery	2	16.000	8.6
Energy planning	1	1.500	0.8
Total	38	185.879	100.0

SOURCE: OPEC data submitted to IBRD meeting on Assistance to the Energy Sector in Developing Countries, Paris, June 25-26, 1979.

UNITED NATIONS DEVELOPMENT PROGRAMME (UNDP)

AND

UNITED NATIONS CENTRE FOR NATURAL RESOURCES, ENERGY AND TRANSPORT (CNRET)

The UNDP, as the primary development financing agency of the U.N. system, has greatly increased its emphasis on energy projects in recent years (although—more than with other agencies—this shift genuinely reflects a change in the interests and priorities of host governments). As of June 30, 1976, the UNDP had 136 active energy projects, with a total UNDP commitment of $49.7 million. As the table below shows, by January 1979 these figures had increased to 179 projects, with a UNDP investment of $136.4 million. Most of these projects support some form of technical assistance.

The CNRET is a very small agency, but is included here because of its emphasis on energy planning assistance, and because it has the only "energy mandate" in the U.N. system outside the UNDP and the International Atomic Energy Agency (IAEA).

Most of the projects shown are, in fact, for some form of advisory services, which is what the CNRET exists to provide. And many of these projects are financed by UNDP, to be executed by CNRET, so there is some overlap between the two tables.

Table 4E. UNDP (as of January 1979)

Type of Project	No. of Projects	Amount ($US Millions)	% of Total Energy Financing
Electric power	36	54.10	39.62
Rural electrification	4	0.74	0.54
Fossil fuels recovery	42	22.80	16.70
Nuclear energy	28	16.80	12.30
Energy planning	35	13.40	9.81
Renewable energy	9	3.30	2.42
Forestry/fuelwood	6	15.30	11.21
Geothermal energy	19	10.10	7.40
Total	179	136.54	100.00

SOURCE: *Cross-Organizational Analysis of the Energy Programs of the United Nations System*, U.N. Document E/AC.51/99, April 23, 1979.

Table 4F.   CNRET (as of January 1979)

Type of Project	No. of Projects	Amount ($US Millions)	% of Total Energy Financing
Electric power	10	2.470	14.3
Rural electrification	1	0.180	1.0
Fossil fuels recovery	10	5.390	31.3
Nuclear energy	0	0	0
Energy planning	9	5.030	29.2
Renewable energy	1	0.076	0.4
Forestry/Fuelwood	0	0	0
Geothermal energy	6	4.090	23.7
Total	37	17.236	100.0

SOURCE: *Cross-Organizational Analysis of the Energy Programs of the United Nations System*, U.N. Document E/AC.51/99, April 23, 1979.

EUROPEAN DEVELOPMENT FUND (EDF)

The European Community's energy aid can be made available through one of four directorates in the Community Secretariat, as described in Chapter 3 (p. 55). Direct project financing ordinarily originates in the EDF, which provides grant aid as well as concessional loans. The official currency of the EDF is a "European Unit of Account" (EUA), one of which equals about 1.35 1979 U.S. dollars.

Before 1975, EDF energy assistance was limited, usually tied to infrastructure projects. This situation has changed quite rapidly, however, and during 1979 the EDF (and the other relevant Community Directorates) have been carrying out an extensive reconsideration of energy aid policy.

EDF project financing procedures combine characteristics of bilateral and multilateral aid. In particular, although grants and loans are highly concessional, relatively strict economic and financial criteria are used for project evaluation. In other words, the EDF evaluates projects as though it were a development bank, but distributes funds more in the manner of a bilateral aid agency.

Table 4G.   EDF (current projects as of May 1978)

Type of Project	No. of Projects	Amount ($US Millions)	% of Total Energy Financing
Power generation			
Hydroelectric	9	122.97	82.20
Thermal	2	8.98	6.00
Subtotal	11	131.95	88.20
Transmission and Distribution			
Rural Electrification	2	2.84	1.90
Other	2	5.74	3.89
Fossil fuels recovery	0	0	0
Nuclear energy	0	0	0
Renewable energy	11	3.42	2.30
Geothermal energy	1	5.53	3.70
Totals	27	149.48	100.00

SOURCES:
"Energy in the ACP States" a special report in *The Courier* (a journal of the European Community–ACP States), September–October 1978.

Cooperation with Developing Countries in the Field of Energy, Commission of the European Communities, COM(78) 355 final, July 31, 1978.

CANADIAN INTERNATIONAL DEVELOPMENT
AGENCY (CIDA)

CIDA's energy program is concentrated in three areas: (1) energy production (including hydroelectric and thermal power stations, electric transmission and distribution projects, rural electrification, and natural gas production); (2) energy resource evaluation; and (3) energy policy development and sector management. The energy program for the period 1972–1982 amounts of $CAN 700.8 million ($US 609.4 million). In 1978/79, disbursements in the energy sector amounted to $CAN 41.8 million ($US 36.3 million), of which at least 90 percent was for hydroelectric projects and transmission lines. Estimated disbursements in 1979/80 will be $CAN 59.3 million ($US 51.6 million). With a similar distribution of priorities, CIDA's energy sector program accounted for 9 percent of bilateral disbursements in 1978/79 and 11 percent in 1979/80.

In Commonwealth Africa, energy projects are primarily in hydroelectric or transmission facilities, although CIDA is participating in rural development projects in Kenya and Lesotho. In Francophone Africa, all current investment is in hydroelectric and transmission facilities.

In Asia and in Latin America, a large percentage of the energy program is concentrated in transmission lines and hydroelectric development. However, CIDA is assisting Bangladesh and Pakistan in natural gas exploration. In Haiti, CIDA has funded a study of hydropower resources and urban electrification based on oil.

Table 4H.1. CIDA's Energy Aid by Region (1978/79 and 1979/80)

	No. of Projects/ Programs	Amount ($US Millions)	Sectoral Energy Aid as % of Regional Total
Asia			
Power generation			
Hydroelectric	7	23.15	57.0
Other	3	1.44	3.5
Transmission & distribution			
Rural electrification	2	5.15	12.7
Other[a]	13	9.72	23.9
Power sector studies	4	0.61	1.5
Fossil fuels recovery	0	0	0
Tech. assis./Energy planning	4	0.20	0.5
Renewable energy[c]	3	0.37	0.9
Fuelwood[c]	0	0	0
Regional Total	36	40.64	100.0 (44.4% of total CIDA Energy aid)
Latin America			
Power generation			
Hydroelectric	1	0.36	8.7
Other	0	0	0
Transmission & distribution			
Rural electrification	0	0	0
Other	1	0.68	16.5
Power sector studies	2	2.58	62.6
Fossil fuels recovery	0	0	0
Tech. assis./Energy planning	1	0.15	3.6
Renewable energy[c]	0	0	0
Fuelwood[c]	2	0.35	8.5
Regional Total	7	4.12	100.0 (4.5% of total CIDA Energy aid)

Commonwealth Africa

Power generation			
Hydroelectric	1	16.40	69.3
Other	0	0	0
Transmission & distribution			
Rural electrification	3	2.30	9.7
Other	10	3.09	13.1
Power sector studies	2	0.39	1.6
Fossil fuels recovery	0	0	0
Tech. assis./Energy planning	2	0.26	1.1
Renewable energy[a]	2	0.21	0.9
Fuelwood[a]	7	1.02	4.3
Regional Total	27	23.67	100.0 (25.9% of total CIDA Energy aid)

Francophone Africa

Power generation			
Hydroelectric	1	1.770	7.7
Other	0	0	0
Transmission & distribution			
Rural electrification	1	0.026	0.1
Other[b]	10	20.520	89.0
Power sector studies	1	0.170	0.7
Fossil fuels recovery	0	0	0
Tech.assis./Energy planning	1	0.034	0.1
Renewable energy[c]	0	0	0
Fuelwood[c]	4	0.520	2.3
Regional Total	18	23.040	100.0 (25.2% of total CIDA Energy aid)

SOURCES:
CIDA data submitted to IBRD meeting on Assistance to the Energy Sector in Developing Countries, Paris, June 25–26, 1979. Annex to *Report by the Working Party of the OECD Council to Develop a Coordinated Effort to Help Developing Countries Bring into Use Technologies Related to Renewable Energy*.

[a] Includes "special line of credit" ($2.0 million) for OGDC, Pakistan.
[b] Includes $13 million loan to CIMAO (Togo).
[c] "Renewable energy" and "Fuelwood" include projects of Canadian International Development Research Centre (IDRC).

Table 4H.2.   CIDA's Energy Aid by Sector Grand Totals (1978/79 and 1979/80)

All Regions	No. of Projects/ Programs	Amount ($US Millions)	Sectoral Energy Aid as % of Grand Total
Power generation			
Hydroelectric	10	41.680	45.60
Other	3	1.440	1.60
Transmission & distribution			
Rural electrification	6	7.476	8.20
Other	34	34.010	37.20
Power sector studies	9	3.750	4.10
Fossil fuels recovery	0	0	0
Tech.assis./Energy planning	8	0.644	0.70
Renewable energy[c]	5	0.580	0.60
Fuelwood[c]	13	1.890	2.00
Grand Totals	88	91.470	100.00

SOURCES:
CIDA data submitted to IBRD meeting on Assistance to the Energy Sector in Developing Countries, Paris, June 25–26, 1979.
Annex to *Report by the Working Party of the OECD Council to Develop a Coordinated Effort to Help Developing Countries Bring into Use Technologies Related to Renewable Energy.*

[a] Includes "special line of credit" ($2.0 million) for OGDC, Pakistan.
[b] Includes $13 million loan to CIMAO (Togo).
[c] "Renewable energy" and "Fuelwood" include projects of Canadian International Development Research Centre (IDRC).

FRENCH BILATERAL ASSISTANCE

The French bilateral aid program is concentrated in francophone countries. Aid for Africa, and francophone countries located in other parts of the world, is administered in the Ministère de la Coopération (Ministry of Cooperation), where the emphasis falls on Sahelian countries. Aid for East Asia and Latin America is handled by the Ministère des Affaires Etrangères (Foreign Ministry).

Technical development of, and international cooperation regarding, solar energy centers in the Commissariat à l'Energie Solaire (COMES). Aid disbursements are given from the Caisse Centrale ("Fund for Aid and Cooperation"—FAC).

The Ministry of Cooperation annually disburses approximately 500 million francs ($120 million) for aid in Africa. About one-third of this is allocated to Sahelian Africa. As the table below indicates, the renewable energy program in West Africa (most projects are in the Sahel) has undertaken sixty-nine projects, disbursing $22.8 million (93.6 million francs) between 1976 and 1979.

Table 41.1. French Energy Aid by Region (1976–1979)

	No. of Projects/ Programs	Amount ($US Millions)	Sectoral Energy Aid as % of Regional Total
Francophone Africa			
Power generation (including studies)			
Hydroelectric	6	149.00	61.9
Other	4	26.20	10.9
Transmission & distribution (including studies)			
Rural electrification	0	0	0
Other	7	34.40	14.3
Fossil fuels recovery	0	0	0
Tech. assis./Energy planning	2	4.90	2.0
Renewable energy			
Research/Development[a]	23	5.83	2.4
Application/Production	46	17.00	7.1
Fuelwood	1	3.40	1.4
Regional totals	89	240.73	100.0 (86% of total French energy aid)
Commonwealth Africa and Other Africa			
Power generation (including studies)			
Hydroelectric	0	0	0
Other	0	0	0
Transmission & distribution (including studies)			
Rural electrification	0	0	0

Other	1	2.9	74.4
Fossil fuels recovery	0	0	0
Tech. assis./Energy planning	0	0	0
Renewable energy			
Research/Development[a]	4	0.2	5.1
Application/Production	5	0.8	20.5
Fuelwood	0	0	0
Regional total	10	3.9	100.0 (1.4% of total French energy aid)
Latin American and Caribbean			
Power generation (including studies)			
Hydroelectric	0	0	0
Other	0	0	0
Transmission & distribution (including studies)			
Rural electrification	0	0	0
Other	0	0	0
Fossil fuels recovery	0	0	0
Tech. assis./Energy planning	9	0.400	91.5
Renewable energy			
Research/Development[a]	1	0.037	8.5
Application/Production	0	0	0
Fuelwood			
Regional totals	10	0.437	100.0 (.2% of total French energy aid)
Asia and Pacific			
Power generation (including studies)			
Hydroelectric	0	0	0
Other	0	0	0

continued

Table 41.1 continued

	No. of Projects/ Programs	Amount ($US Millions)	Sectoral Energy Aid as % of Regional Total
Transmission & distribution (including studies)			
Rural electrification	2	7.40	41.6
Other	10	9.00	50.6
Fossil fuels recovery	0	0	0
Tech. assis./Energy planning	0	0	0
Renewable energy			
Research/Development[a]	11	1.20	6.7
Application/Production	3	0.19	1.1
Fuelwood	0	0	0
Regional totals	26	17.79	100.0 (6.4% of total French energy aid)
Middle East and Europe			
Power generation (including studies)			
Hydroelectric	0	0	0
Other	0	0	0
Transmission & distribution (including studies)			
Rural electrification	0	0	0
Other	0	0	0
Fossil fuels recovery	0	0	0
Tech. assis./Energy planning	0	0	0
Renewable energy			
Research/Development[a]	3	0.030	55.6
Application/Production	1	0.024	44.4
Fuelwood	0	0	0
Regional total	4	0.054	100.0 (less than .1% of total French energy aid)

Regional and Global			*Sectoral energy aid as* % of regional and global total
Power generation (including studies)			
Hydroelectric	0	0	0
Other	0	0	0
Transmission & distribution (including studies)			
Rural electrification	0	0	0
Other	0	0	0
Fossil fuels recovery	4	15.60	92.1
Tech. assis./Energy planning	0	0	0
Renewable energy			
Research/Development[a]	2	1.34	7.9
Application/Production	0	0	0
Fuelwood	0	0	0
Regional and global projects totals	6	16.94	100.0 (6.1% of total French energy aid)

SOURCES:
French data submitted to IBRD meeting on Assistance to the Energy Sector in Developing Countries, Paris, June 25–26, 1979.
Annual reports, Caisse Centrale de Coopération Économique, 1976, 1977, 1978.
Interviews with Ministère de la Coopération and the Commissariat à l'Énergie Solaire (COMES).
[a]Includes technical assistance and studies for renewable energy.

Table 41.1.   French Energy Aid by Sector, Grand Totals (1976–1979)

	No. of Projects/ Programs	Amount ($US Millions)	Sectoral Energy Aid as % of Grand Total
All Regions			
Power generation (including studies)			
Hydroelectric	6	149.000	53.2
Other	4	26.200	9.4
Transmission & distribution (including studies)			
Rural electrification	2	7.400	2.6
Other	18	46.300	16.5
Fossil fuels recovery	4	15.600	5.6
Tech. assis./Energy planning	2	4.900	1.8
Research/Development[a]	52	9.000	3.2
Application/Production	56	18.051	6.5
Fuelwood	1	3.400	1.2
Grand totals	145	279.851	100.0

SOURCES:
French data submitted to IBRD meeting on Assistance to the Energy Sector in Developing Countries, Paris, June 25–26, 1979.
Annual reports, Caisse Centrale de Coopération Économique, 1976, 1977, 1978.
Interviews with Ministère de la Coopération and the Commissariat à l'Énergie Solaire (COMES).

FEDERAL REPUBLIC OF GERMANY

MINISTRY OF ECONOMIC COOPERATION (BMZ)

The German aid program is administered through two distinct agencies within the ministry. The Kreditanstalt für Wiederaufbau (KfW) handles capital aid projects and up to now has been organized along regional lines. The Agency for Technical Cooperation (Gesellschaft für Technische Zusammenarbeit, or GTZ) handles technical assistance projects and recently established a new division, the German Appropriate Technology Exchange (GATE), which will handle most renewable energy projects.

In part due to a lack of recent ex-colonial links comparable to those of Britain, France, or the Netherlands, German aid has traditionally focused on middle-income developing countries. These tables reflect that focus, showing a concentration of energy aid in the Middle East and North Africa. The German aid program is, however, moving toward a strategy of "aid for the poorest," so new energy projects may be targeted differently.

Table 4J.1.   German Energy Aid by Region (1970-present)

	No. of Projects/ Programs Committed	(No. of Projects/ Programs Planned)ᵃ	Amount Committed ($US Millions)	(Amount Planned— $US Millions)ᵇ	Sectoral Energy Aid as % of Regional Total (Committed only)
Africa					
Power generation (including studies)					
Hydroelectric	10	(3)	252.590	(51.950)	61.2
Other (including fuel provision)	6	(1)	8.870	(1.390)	2.1
Transmission, distribution, and plant rehabilitation (including studies)					
Rural electrification	2	(2)	11.800	(8.000)	2.9
Other	20	(11)	104.606	(66.450)	25.3
Fossil fuels recovery (including studies)	1	(1)	2.300	(2.220)	0.6
Tech. assis./Energy planning	12	(2)	10.285	(1.745)	2.5
Renewable energy (including studies)	10	(7)	5.670	(8.780)	1.4
Forestry (GTZ)ᶜ	11		16.870		4.0
Regional total	72	(27)	412.991	(140.535)	100.0 (19.7% of total German energy aid)
Asia					
Power generation (including studies)					
Hydroelectric	6	(2)	30.020	(38.90)	7.2
Other (including fuel provision)	4	(1)	134.100	(47.20)	32.2

Transmission, distribution, and plant rehabilitation (including studies)				
Rural electrification	0	(1)	0	(18.90)
Other	19	(9)	231.557	(81.26)
Fossil fuels recovery (including studies)	2	(3)	5.820	(18.70)
Tech. assis./Energy planning	9	(1)	9.790	(1.50)
Renewable energy (including studies)	7	(5)	1.950	(7.09)
Forestry (GTZ)^c	4		3.150	
Regional total	51	(22)	416.387	(213.55)

Rural electrification	0
Other	55.6
Fossil fuels recovery (including studies)	1.4
Tech. assis./Energy planning	2.4
Renewable energy (including studies)	0.5
Forestry (GTZ)^c	0.7
Regional total	100.0 (19.9% of total German energy aid)

Latin American and Caribbean

Power generation (including studies)				
Hydroelectric	7	(3)	84.571	(30.70)
Other (including fuel provision)	7	(3)	92.700	(25.00)
Transmission, distribution, and plant rehabilitation (including studies)				
Rural electrification	0	(1)	0	(8.30)
Other	8	(5)	45.020	(82.70)
Fossil fuels recovery (including studies)	2	(2)	1.474	(1.66)
Tech. assis./Energy planning	6	(2)	17.660	(1.12)
Renewable energy (including studies)	4	(5)	3.998	(7.51)
Forestry (GTZ)^c	3		7.790	
Regional total	37	(21)	253.213	(156.99)

Hydroelectric	33.4
Other (including fuel provision)	36.6
Rural electrification	0
Other	17.8
Fossil fuels recovery (including studies)	0.6
Tech. assis./Energy planning	7.0
Renewable energy (including studies)	1.6
Forestry (GTZ)^c	3.0
Regional total	100.0 (12.1% of total German energy aid)

continued

Table 4J.1 continued

	No. of Projects/ Programs Committed	(No. of Projects/ Programs Planned)[a]	Amount Committed ($US Millions)	(Amount Planned— $US Millions)[b]	Sectoral Energy Aid as % of Regional Total (Committed only)
Europe, Middle East and North Africa					
Power generation (including studies)					
Hydroelectric	5	(3)	107.820	(4.42)	10.9
Other (including fuel provision)	12	(5)	403.500	(261.46)	40.7
Transmission, distribution, and plant rehabilitation (including studies)					
Rural electrification	1	(2)	13.900	(26.70)	1.4
Other	20	(5)	403.657	(29.30)	40.9
Fossil fuels recovery (including studies)	3	(1)	30.580	(19.40)	3.1
Tech. Assis./Energy planning	8		9.467		1.0
Renewable energy (including studies)	11	(2)	13.396	(1.20)	1.4
Forestry (GTZ)[c]	4		5.580		0.6
Regional total	64	(18)	987.900	(342.48)	100.0 (47.2% of total German energy aid)

Regional and Global					*Sectoral Energy Aid as % of Regional and Global Total (Committed only)*
Power generation (including studies)					
Hydroelectric	1		0.008		less than 0.1
Other (including fuel provision)	0		0		0
Transmission, distribution, and plant rehabilitation					
Rural electrification	0		0		0
Other	0		0		0
Fossil fuels recovery (including studies)	2		0.657		2.7
Tech. assis./Energy planning	7	(1)	0.781	(0.056)	3.2
Renewable energy (including studies)	28	(10)	23.002	(14.366)	94.1
Forestry GTZ[c]	0		0		0
Regional and Global projects totals	38	(11)	24.448	(14.422)	100.0 (1.1% of total German energy aid)

SOURCES:
German data submitted to IBRD meeting on Assistance to the Energy Sector in Developing Countries, Paris, June 25–26, 1979. Annex to *Report by the Working Party of the OECD Council to Develop a Coordinated Effort to Help Developing Countries Bring into Use Technologies Related to Renewable Energy.*
Interviews with German government officials.

[a]Numbers in parentheses indicate the number of additional projects planned (funds for these not yet committed) in each sector, based on BMZ projections in November 1979.

[b]Numbers in parentheses indicate the amount of additional expenditures planned (but not yet committed) in each sector, based on BMZ projections in November 1979.

[c]No information available to indicate what percentage of forestry projects are meant primarily for fuelwood production.

Table 4J.2.   German Energy Aid by Sector, Grand Totals (1970–present)

	No. of Projects/ Programs Committed	(No. of Projects/ Programs Planned)[a]	Amount Committed ($US Millions)	(Amount Planned— $US Millions)[b]	Sectoral Energy Aid as % of Grand Total (committed only)
All Regions					
Power generation (including studies)					
Hydroelectric	29	(11)	475.009	(125.970)	22.7
Other (including fuel provision)	29	(10)	639.170	(335.050)	30.5
Transmission, distribution, and plant rehabilitation (including studies)					
Rural electrification	3	(6)	25.700	(61.900)	1.2
Other	67	(30)	784.840	(259.710)	37.5
Fossil fuels recovery (including studies)	10	(8)	40.831	(42.036)	1.9
Tech. assis./Energy planning	42	(5)	47.983	(4.365)	2.3
Renewable energy (including studies)	60	(29)	48.016	(38.946)	2.3
Forestry (GTZ)[c]	22		33.390		1.6
Grand totals	262	(99)	2,094.939	(867.977)	100.0

SOURCES:
German data submitted to IBRD meeting on Assistance to the Energy Sector in Developing Countries, Paris, June 25-26, 1979. *Annex to Report by the Working Party of the OECD Council to Develop a Coordinated Effort to Help Developing Countries Bring into Use Technologies Related to Renewable Energy.* Interviews with German government officials.

[a] Numbers in parentheses indicate the number of additional projects planned (funds for these not yet committed) in each sector, based on BMZ projections in November 1979.

[b] Numbers in parentheses indicate the amount of additional expenditures planned (but not yet committed) in each sector, based on BMZ projections in November 1979.

[c] No information available to indicate what percentage of forestry projects are meant primarily for fuelwood production.

KUWAIT FUND FOR ARAB
ECONOMIC DEVELOPMENT

Established in 1962, the Kuwait Fund is the oldest and largest of the Arab development assistance institutions. The Fund has a working capital of $3.45 billion and is empowered by its charter to borrow up to two times its capital base.

From its inception in 1962 through FY 1978, the Kuwait Fund has committed $1.945 billion in 131 loans to over forty countries. Until 1974 the Fund's activities were limited to the Arab world; since then, 48 percent of all loans have gone to Asia and non-Arab Africa. Kuwait Fund loans carry an interest rate of 1.5–4 percent with a five-year grace period and between nineteen and thirty-four years for final maturities.

Most loans in the power sector have been for rural electrification, hydroelectric, and thermal power projects. From FY 1962 to FY 1978, 28 percent of the Fund's loans have gone to the electric power sector. In FY 1978 loans to the electric power sector increased to 30 percent.

Table 4K.   Kuwait Fund (FY 1973–FY 1978)

Type of Project	No. of Projects	Amount ($US Millions)	% of Total Energy Financing
Power generation			
Hydroelectric	8	200.9	37.50
Thermal	7	142.1	26.50
Subtotal	15	343.0	64.00
Transmission and distribution			
Rural electrification	2	25.9	4.80
Other	3	68.0	12.70
Fossil fuels recovery	5	98.6	18.40
Nuclear energy	0	0	0
Renewable energy	1	0.8	0.15
Geothermal energy	0	0	0
Total	26	536.3	100.00

SOURCE: Annual Reports FY 1973–FY 1978.

THE NETHERLANDS

MINISTRY OF FOREIGN AFFAIRS, DIRECTORATE GENERAL FOR

INTERNATIONAL COOPERATION (DGIC)

The Dutch aid program is unique in many respects. It has access to an unusually high percentage of GNP, which the Netherlands devotes to aid programs. In 1977 the Dutch devoted about .85 percent of their gross national product (GNP) to aid, the second highest of all DAC countries behind Sweden (which gave .99 percent in 1977). The DGIC is run by an extremely small staff who rely heavily on the technical expertise of outside, quasi-governmental institutes and specialized universities.

The historical distribution of Dutch aid for energy parallels that of other agencies in its concentration on modern-sector electrification. However, in late 1979 the Netherlands became the first (and so far, only) aid donor to establish a comprehensive energy assistance policy that pledges to redirect programs and reallocate funds (see text, p. 65). This includes a pledge to devote 25 million guilders ($13.2 million) "over the next few years" to research on the application of renewable energy sources in developing countries, and to spend 100 million guilders ($52.6 million) annually on afforestation and promotion of wood-use efficiency.

Table 4L.1.   Dutch Development Cooperation—Energy Aid by Region (1970–present)

	No. of Projects/ Programs	Amount ($US Millions)	Sectoral Energy Aid as % of Regional Total
Africa			
Power generation (including studies)			
Hydroelectric	0	0	0
Other	2	8.50	42.4
Transmission & distribution (including studies)			
Rural electrification	1	4.75	23.7
Other	3	3.56	17.7
Fossil fuels recovery	2	1.54	7.7
Tech. assis./Energy planning	1	0.28	1.4
Renewable energy	6	1.43	7.1
Fuelwood[a]	—	—	—
Regional total	15	20.06	100.0 (10.1% of total Dutch energy aid)
Asia			
Power generation (including studies)			
Hydroelectric	1	0.38	0.2
Other	4	25.43	16.5
Transmission & distribution (including studies)			
Rural electrification	6	37.53	24.4
Other	6	17.66	11.5
Fossil fuels recovery	4	69.30	45.1
Tech. assis./Energy planning	1	0.49	0.3
Renewable energy	7	2.95	1.9
Fuelwood[a]	—	—	—
Regional total	29	153.74	100.0 (77.6% of total Dutch energy aid)

continued

Table 4L.1 continued

	No. of Projects/ Programs	Amount ($US Millions)	Sectoral Energy Aid as % of Regional and Global Total
Latin America and Caribbean			
Power generation (including studies)			
Hydroelectric	1	7.510	63.2
Other	1	3.200	26.9
Transmission & distribution (including studies)			
Rural electrification	1	0.400	3.4
Other	1	.023	0.2
Fossil fuels recovery	0	0	0
Tech. assis./Energy planning	1	0.750	6.3
Renewable energy	0	0	0
Fuelwood[a]	—	—	—
Regional total	5	11.883	100.0 (6% of total Dutch energy aid)
Europe, Middle East, and North Africa			
Power generation (including studies)			
Hydroelectric	0	0	0
Other	0	0	0
Transmission & distribution (including studies)			
Rural electrification	0	0	0
Other	1	10.242	90.5
Fossil fuels recovery	0	0	0
Tech. assis./Energy planning	0	0	0

Renewable energy			
Fuelwood[a]	3	1.073	9.5
Regional total	4	11.315	100.0 (5.7% of total Dutch energy aid)
Regional and Global			
Power generation (including studies)			
Hydroelectric	0	0	0
Other	0	0	0
Transmission & distribution (including studies)			
Rural electrification	0	0	0
Other	0	0	0
Fossil fuels recovery	0	0	0
Tech. assis./Energy planning	0	0	0
Renewable energy	2	1.1	100
Fuelwood			
Regional and global projects totals	2	1.1	100 (.6% of total Dutch energy aid)

SOURCES:
Netherlands' Development Cooperation Agency Project List—Bilateral Aid Energy Projects in Developing Countries, October 1979.
Netherlands' Development Cooperation Policy 1979—presentation of foreign affairs budget to Parliament.
[a]No information on Dutch aid activities in fuelwood was available for inclusions in these charts.

Table 4L.2.   Dutch Development Cooperation—Energy Aid by Sector, Grand Totals (1970-present)

	No. of Projects/ Programs	Amount ($US Millions)	Sectoral Energy Aid as % of Grand Total
All Regions			
Power generation (including studies)			
Hydroelectric	2	7.890	4.0
Other	7	37.130	18.7
Transmission & Distribution (including studies)			
Rural electrification	8	42.680	21.5
Other	11	31.485	15.9
Fossil fuels recovery	6	70.840	35.8
Tech. assis./Energy planning	3	1.520	0.8
Renewable energy	18	6.553	3.3
Fuelwood[a]	—	—	
Grand totals	55	198.098	100.0

SOURCES:
Netherlands' Development Cooperation Agency Project List—Bilateral Aid Energy Projects in Developing Countries, October 1979.
Netherlands' Development Cooperation Policy 1979—presentation of foreign affairs budget to Parliament.
[a]No information on Dutch aid activities in fuelwood was available for inclusion in these charts.

UNITED KINGDOM

OVERSEAS DEVELOPMENT ADMINISTRATION (ODA)

Electric power generation, transmission, and management have been the principal focus of the United Kingdom's energy aid program. The Overseas Development Administration (formerly the Ministry for Overseas Development) has funded feasibility studies and technical assistance, as well as providing foreign exchange for construction projects. In 1975 £16.4 million ($37.4 million) were dispersed on bilateral energy projects, out of total ODM disbursements that year of £119.9 million ($273.4 million).

During 1978 ODA began to show some interest in renewable energy projects, in order to bring its energy program into line with its overall "aid to the poorest" strategy. Technical Working Groups were established to study the possibilities of applying solar, wind and wave, and biomass energy systems.

Table 4M.1.   U.K. ODA Energy Aid[a] by Region (1973–present)

	No. of Projects/Programs	Amount ($US Millions)	Sectoral Energy Aid as % of Regional Total
Africa			
Power generation, transmission, and distribution (including studies)			
Hydroelectric	4	65.73	93.6
Other	1	4.20	6.0
Fossil fuels recovery	0	0	0
Tech. assis./Energy planning	0	0	0
Renewable energy			
Research/Development[b]	4	0.28	0.4
Application/Production	0	0	0
Fuelwood	0	0	0
Regional total	9	70.21	100.0 (47% of total U.K. energy aid)
Asia and Pacific			
Power generation, transmission, and distribution (including studies)			
Hydroelectric	5	62.600	84.0
Other	2	11.200	15.0
Fossil fuels recovery	1	0.530	0.7
Tech. assis./Energy planning	0	0	0
Renewable energy			
Research/Development[b]	3	0.160	0.2
Application/Production	2	0.015	less than 1.0
Fuelwood	0	0	0
Regional total	13	74.505	100.0 (49.9% of total U.K. energy aid)

Latin America and Caribbean

			Sectoral Energy Aid as % of Regional and Global Total
Power generation, transmission, and distribution (including studies)			
Hydroelectric	1	1.890	50.6
Other	0	0	0
Fossil fuels recovery	0	0	0
Tech. Assis./Energy planning	1	0.105	2.8
Renewable energy			
Research/Development[b]	4	1.740	46.6
Application/Production	0	0	0
Fuelwood	0	0	0
Regional totals	6	3.735	100.0 (2.5% of total U.K. energy aid)

Regional and Global

Power generation, transmission, and distribution (including studies)			
Hydroelectric	0	0	0
Other	0	0	0
Fossil fuels recovery	0	0	0
Tech. assis./Energy planning	0	0	0
Renewable energy			
Research/Development[b]	18	0.92	100
Application/Production	0	0	0
Fuelwood	0	0	0
Regional and global projects totals	18	0.92	100 (.6% of total U.K. energy aid)

SOURCES:
Interviews at Overseas Development Administration Science and Technology Department.
U.K. data submitted to IBRD meeting on Assistance to the Energy Sector in Developing Countries, Paris, June 25-26, 1979.
[a] Includes projects financed from ODA funds and administered by other agencies (ITDG, etc.).
[b] Includes technical assistance and studies for renewable energy.

Table 4M.2.   U.K. ODA Energy Aid by Sector, Grand Totals[a] (1973–present)

All Regions	No. of Projects/ Programs	Amount ($US Millions)	Sectoral Energy Aid as % of Grand Total
Power generation, transmission, and distribution (including studies)			
Hydroelectric	10	130.220	87.2
Other	3	15.400	10.3
Fossil fuels recovery	1	0.530	0.4
Tech. assis./Energy planning	1	0.105	less than 1.0
Renewable energy			
Research/Development[b]	29	3.100	2.1
Application/Production	2	0.015	less than 1.0
Fuelwood	0	0	0
Grand totals	46	149.370	100.0

SOURCES:
Interviews at Overseas Development Administration Science and Technology Department.
U.K. data submitted to IBRD meetings on Assistance to the Energy Sector in Developing Countries, Paris, June 25–26, 1979.
[a] Includes projects financed from ODA funds and administered by other agencies (ITDG, etc.).
[b] Includes technical assistance and studies for renewable energy.

UNITED STATES

AGENCY FOR INTERNATIONAL DEVELOPMENT (AID)

The U.S. AID energy program is moving toward an emphasis on the development of renewable energy sources, assessment of LDC energy resources, and strengthening of LDC institutions to provide a better base for formulation and implementation of LDC energy policies. This change of emphasis in AID's energy programs was produced by the 1973 "new direction" policy, which endeavors to channel assistance directly to the poorest, and by 1977 amendments to the Foreign Assistance Act that added a mandate to provide assistance for renewable energy systems.

Major categories of AID's renewable energy program are (1) energy production (including production of charcoal), development of village woodlots, and use of solar energy devices; (2) energy resource evaluation, including a study of deforestation for firewood in Africa and survey of available renewable resources in Latin America; and (3) energy policy development and sector management (including forestry management in Africa), energy sector studies planned for the Central American region, and extensive technology R & D training in renewable resources in Asia and the Near East.

Although official policy indicates that AID should be shifting away from rural electrification, at this time such a trend is discernible only in the number of projects started each year; it has not yet had a major effect on the total obligations. Rural electrification project starts numbered four in FY 1978, three in FY 1979, and only one in FY 1980. Obligations in that time remained fairly steady, from $72.8 million in FY 1978, to $82.6 million in FY 1979 to $80.0 million in FY 1980. Over time, a decrease in new project starts should result in some decrease in the amounts obligated for rural electrification projects.

Table 4N.1. U.S. AID Energy Aid by Region (FY 1978–FY 1980) Current–Committed

	FY 1978		FY 1979		FY 1980 (projected)		Totals	
	No. of Projects[a]	Amount ($Millions)	No. of Projects[a]	Amount ($Millions)	No. of Projects[a]	Amount ($Millions)	No. of Projects[a]	Amount ($Millions)
Asia								
Power generation	0	0	0	0	0	0	0	0
Rural electrification	3	62.65	3	74.000	1	11.000	7	147.650
Fossil fuels recovery	0	0	0	0	0	0	0	0
Tech. assis./ Energy planning	1	1.30	1	1.330	6	7.100	8	9.730
Renewables R & D	1	5.00	3	9.285	2	5.135	6	19.420
Renewables Application/ Production	0	0	4	7.412	0	0	4	7.412
Fuelwood	0	0	0	0	1	0.700	1	0.700
Regional total	5	68.95	11	92.027	10	23.935	26	184.912
Latin America								
Power generation	1	0.085	1	0.085	0	0	2	0.170
Rural electrification	1	10.000	2	8.621	1	69.00	4	87.621
Fossil fuels recovery	0	0	0	0	0	0	0	0
Tech. assis./ Energy planning	3	0.962	8	1.985	5	7.71	16	10.657
Renewables R & D	0	0	3	0.980	2	0.58	5	1.560
Renewables Application/ Production	0	0	1	0.400	1	3.00	2	3.400
Fuelwood	0	0	0	0	0	0	0	0
Regional total	5	11.047	15	12.071	9	80.29	29	103.408

Africa

Power generation	0	0	0	0	0	0	0	0
Rural electrification	0	0	0	0	0	0	0	0
Fossil fuels recovery	0	0	0	0	0	0	0	0
Tech. assis./ Energy planning	2	0.230	2	0.570	2	0.129	6	0.929
Renewables R & D	5	5.563	5	1.954	3	1.500	13	9.017
Renewables Application/ Production	1	0.700	1	0.450	1	0.480	3	1.630
Fuelwood	3	1.090	5	1.470	5	4.097	13	6.657
Regional total	11	7.583	13	4.444	11	6.206	35	18.233

Europe, Middle East, and North Africa

Power generation	2	46.000[b]	1	100.00[b]	1	3.00[b]	4	149.000
Rural electrification	1	18.050[b]	0	0	0	0	1	18.050
Fossil fuels recovery	1	0.158	1	0.12	0	0	2	0.278
Tech. assis./ Energy planning	0	0	2	1.37[b]	1	1.50[b]	3	2.870
Renewables R & D	1	0.042[b]	1	2.00	2	20.25[b]	4	22.292
Renewables Application/ Production	0	0	0	0	0	0	0	0
Fuelwood	0	0	0	0	0	0	0	0
Regional total	5	64.250	5	103.49	4	24.75	14	192.490

Regional and Global Projects

Power generation	0	0	0	0	0	0	0	0
Rural electrification	1	0.200	0	0	0	0	1	0.200
Fossil fuels recovery	0	0	0	0	1	1.900	1	1.900
Tech. assis./ Energy planning	2	0.707	8	8.515	7	12.350	17	21.572

continued

Table 4N.1. continued

	FY 1978		FY 1979		FY 1980 (projected)		Totals	
	No. of Projects[a]	Amount ($Millions)	No. of Projects[a]	Amount ($Millions)	No. of Projects[a]	Amount ($Millions)	No. of Projects[a]	Amount ($Millions)
Renewables R & D	0	0	6	5.350	7	14.925	13	20.275
Renewables Application/ Production	0	0	0	0	1	1.750	1	1.750
Fuelwood	0	0	2	1.607	0	0	2	1.607
Regional and global projects totals	3	0.907	16	15.472	16	30.925	35	47.304
Grand totals	29	152.737	60	227.504	50	166.106	139	546.347

SOURCES:
AID data submitted to IBRD meeting on Assistance to the Energy Sector in Developing Countries, Paris, 25–26, June 1979.
AID Congressional Presentation FY 1979—Main Vol., Annexes A and B.
AID Congressional Presentation FY 1980—Main Vol., Annex VIII.

[a] Number of projects = projects funded each year (may be continuing projects).
[b] Security Support Assistance.

Table 4N.2.   U.S. AID Energy Aid by Sector, Grand Totals (in $Millions)

All Regions	FY 1978	% of Total Spending FY 1978	FY 1979	% of Total Spending FY 1979	FY 1980	% of Total Spending FY 1980	Total	% of Total Spending for All Years
Power generation	46.085 (0.085)[a]	30.2	100.085 (0.085)[a]	44.00	3.000 (0)[a]	1.89	149.170 (0.170)[a]	27.3
Rural electrification	90.900 (72.850)[a]	59.2	82.621	36.30	80.000	48.20	253.521 (235.471)[a]	46.4
Fossil fuels recovery	0.158	0.1	.120	0.05	1.900	1.10	2.178	0.4
Tech. assis./ Energy planning	3.199	2.1	13.770 (12.400)[a]	6.00	28.789 (27.289)[a]	17.30	45.758 (42.888)[a]	8.4
Renewables R & D	10.605 (10.563)[a]	6.9	19.569	8.67	42.390 (22.140)[a]	25.50	72.564 (52.272)[a]	13.3
Renewables Application/ Production	0.700	0.5	8.262	3.60	5.230	3.10	14.192	2.6
Fuelwood	1.090	0.7	3.077	1.40	4.797	2.90	8.964	1.6
Grand totals	152.737 (88.645)[a]	100.0	227.504 (126.134)[a]	100.00	166.106 (141.356)[a]	100.00	546.347 (356.135)[a]	100.0

SOURCES:
AID data submitted to IBRD meeting on Assistance to the Energy Sector in Developing Countries, Paris, 25–26, June 1979.
AID Congressional Presentation FY 1979—Main Vol., Annexes A and B.
AID Congressional Presentation FY 1980—Main Vol., Annex VIII.
[a]Total for sector if Security Support Assistance were *excluded*.

Table 4 Summary (in $US Millions)

	Conventional Power Generation (Hydro, Nuclear, Thermal), Transmission, Distribution; Power Sector Studies	Fossil Fuels Recovery (Includes studies & training)	New & Renewables (includes Geothermal, Fuelwood)	Tech. Assis./ Energy Planning, Other	Total Energy Aid
World Bank (FY 1972-Dec. 1978)	5,210.400	305.400	170.300	—	5,686.100
Asian Develop. Bank (FY 1972-FY 1978)	1,182.900	20.800	0	—	1,203.700
Inter-American Development Bank (FY 1972-FY 1978)	2,596.100	158.000	4.100	—	2,758.200
OPEC Fund (1977-present)	168.379	16.000	—	1.500	185.879
United Nations Development Programme (to Jan. 1979)	71.640	22.800	28.700	13.400	136.540
United Nations Center for Natural Resources, Energy and Transport (to Jan. 1979)	2.650	5.390	4.166	5.030	17.236
European Develop. Fund (to May 1978)	140.530	0	8.950	—	149.480
Canadian International Develop. Agency (1978/79, 1979/80)	88.356	0	2.470	0.644	91.470
French Aid (1976-1979)	228.900	15.600	30.451	4.900	279.851
German Aid (1970-present)	1,924.719	40.831	81.406	47.983	2,094.939
Kuwait Fund (FY 1973-FY 1978)	436.900	98.600	0.800	—	536.300

Netherlands—Dutch Develop. Cooperation (1970–present)	119.185	70.840	6.553	1.520	198.098
United Kingdom Overseas Development Administration (1973–present)	145.620	0.530	3.115	0.105	149.370
United States Agency for International Development[a] (FY 1978–FY 1980)	402.691	2.178	95.720	45.758	546.347
Grand totals	12,718.97	756.969	436.731	120.840	14,033.51
Percentage in each sector	90.6	5.4	3.1	0.9	100

[a]Includes Security Support Assistance.

TABLE 5

INTERNATIONAL ENERGY AID BY RECIPIENT COUNTRY AND REGION

Table 5 summarizes bilateral and multilateral energy assistance according to recipient country and region. It includes all of the projects reflected in Table 4 (the fourteen major energy donors, for the periods given in Table 4), totaling $14 billion. *It also includes* all energy projects of the U.N. system, and available data on projects of some other major donors (including Japan, New Zealand, Sweden, Switzerland), totaling $3.5 billion, which are not included in Table 4. Table 5 is not, therefore, meant to present a total picture of world energy aid, since for reasons of time and available resources, certain bilateral and OPEC aid programs (as well as smaller multilateral banks) were not included in this study. The comprehensiveness and accuracy of Table 5 may be limited by data-reporting systems of aid donors, but we believe that it provides a good *general picture of comparative order of magnitude* among countries and regions for energy aid projects after 1972.

Table 5 summarizes energy aid project listings compiled by the International Institute for Environment and Development; a copy of the entire list can be obtained by writing to the institute.*

It must be emphasized that Table 5 takes a picture of a moving target: It does not cover one consistent chronological period for all agencies represented. Multilateral agencies compile statistical data on a fiscal year basis (and it is presented in this form in Table 4), whereas the U.N. system presents information on a "current project" basis. Bilateral agencies use both systems: It is possible to examine *budget projections* for many bilateral agencies on a fiscal year basis, but *project disbursements* are more often characterized on the "current project" basis. Finally, the information on multilateral agencies and the U.N. system is publicly available and comprehensive. Bilateral aid statistics are harder to obtain (although this is not true of renewable energy aid, which is well publicized), and as the Development Assistance Committee of the OECD points out, difficult to portray on a comparative basis. *For these reasons, Table 6 tends to be biased in favor of renewable energy projects and in favor of recent projects.*

---

*International Institute for Environment and Development, Suite 501, 1302 Eighteenth Street, N.W., Washington, D.C. 20036.

Table 5A.   Europe, the Middle East, and North Africa

	Project Type	*No. of Projects*	*Amount ($US Millions)*
Afghanistan	Power systems (generation, transmission, distribution)	7	95.539
	Fossil fuels recovery	1	7.300
	Nuclear energy	1	0.023
	Energy planning/ Technical assistance	5	4.900
	Renewable energy	3	0.187
			107.949
Algeria	Power systems	2	96.000
	Fossil fuels recovery	1	27.800
	Energy planning/TA	1	1.107
	Renewable energy	4	2.481
			127.388
Bahrain	Power systems	1	21.89
Cyprus	Energy planning/TA	1	0.158
	Renewable energy	2	0.082
			0.240
Egypt	Power systems	17	546.643
	Fossil fuels recovery	3	108.800
	Energy planning/TA	7	5.995
	Renewable energy	10	25.266
	Forestry/Fuelwood	1	0.096
			686.800
Greece	Fossil fuels recovery	1	100.000
	Nuclear energy	1	0.499
	Energy planning/TA	1	0.025
			100.524
Iceland	Power systems	1	2.2
Iran	Power systems	6	225.22
	Renewable energy	1	0.28
			225.50
Iraq	Power systems	1	54.15
Jordan	Power systems	9	72.600
	Fossil fuels recovery	1	0.360
	Energy planning/TA	3	0.387
	Renewable energy	2	3.080
	Forestry/Fuelwood	1	0.122
	Geothermal energy	1	0.106
			76.655

continued

Table 5A continued

	Project Type	No. of Projects	Amount ($US Millions)
Kuwait	Renewable energy	1	0.17
Malta	Renewable energy	1	3.6
Morocco	Power systems	7	107.405
	Fossil fuels recovery	1	0.780
	Renewable energy	1	2.000
			110.185
Oman	Fossil fuels recovery	1	26.700
	Renewable energy	1	0.024
			26.724
Portugal	Power systems	1	10.700
	Rural electrification	1	13.900
	Renewable energy	1	0.006
			24.606
Saudi Arabia	Energy planning/TA	1	0.023
	Renewable energy	2	50.024
			50.047
Spain	Power systems	1	11.11
Syria	Power systems	7	184.250
	Rural electrification	1	18.050
	Fossil fuels recovery	4	18.553
	Energy planning/TA	1	1.500
			222.353
Tunisia	Power systems	10	96.061
	Rural electrification	2	1.862
	Fossil fuels recovery	4	11.728
	Energy planning/TA	1	0.062
	Renewable energy	2	0.049
	Forestry/Fuelwood	1	0.157
			109.919
Turkey	Power systems	8	349.000
	Fossil fuels recovery	9	329.163
	Nuclear energy	1	0.657
	Energy planning/TA	2	0.634
	Forestry/Fuelwood	1	86.000
			765.454
People's Democratic Republic of Yemen (Aden)			
	Power systems	1	5.0

Table 5A continued

	Project Type	No. of Projects	Amount ($US Millions)
Yemen Arab Republic (Sana)			
	Power systems	2	12.492
	Energy planning/TA	2	1.080
	Renewable energy	1	0.750
			14.322
Yugoslavia	Power systems	1	194.4

Table 5B.   West Africa

	Project Type	No. of Projects	Amount ($US Millions)
Benin	Power systems (generation, transmission, distribution)	3	1.759
	Energy planning/ Technical assistance	1	0.100
	Renewable energy	1	0.027
	Forestry/Fuelwood	3	0.970
			2.856
Cameroon	Power systems	7	97.957
	Nuclear energy	1	0.165
	Energy planning/TA	3	2.660
	Renewable energy	9	17.761
			118.543
Cape Verde	Power systems	2	0.683
	Fossil fuels recovery	1	2.300
	Renewable energy	9	3.765
	Geothermal energy	1	0.070
			6.818
Chad	Power systems	2	3.489
	Fossil fuels recovery	3	4.812
	Renewable energy	5	0.989
	Forestry/Fuelwood	3	0.860
			10.150
Congo	Renewable energy	2	0.724
Gabon	Power systems	3	29.580
	Energy planning/TA	1	2.440
			32.020

continued

Table 5B continued

	Project Type	No. of Projects	Amount ($US Millions)
Gambia	Power systems	4	4.678
	Energy planning/TA	1	1.110
	Renewable energy	2	0.027
	Forestry/Fuelwood	2	0.338
			6.153
Ghana	Power systems	16	242.681
	Energy planning/TA	3	1.920
	Renewable energy	3	1.453
	Forestry/Fuelwood	3	1.459
			247.513
Guinea	Power systems	2	0.532
	Fossil fuels recovery	1	- - - - - - -
	Renewable energy	1	0.212
			0.744
Guinea-Bissau	Energy planning/TA	4	1.987
	Forestry/Fuelwood	1	0.050
			2.037
Ivory Coast	Power systems	7	84.852
	Rural electrification	1	0.022
	Forestry/Fuelwood	1	18.000
			102.874
Liberia	Power systems	6	35.515
	Fossil fuels recovery	1	- - - - - - -
			35.515
Mali	Power systems	11	102.299
	Energy planning/TA	1	0.030
	Renewable energy	10	6.595
	Forestry/Fuelwood	3	2.839
			111.763
Mauritania	Power systems	2	1.095
	Renewable energy	12	3.855
	Forestry/Fuelwood	2	0.459
			5.409
Niger	Power systems	12	34.965
	Fossil fuels recovery	3	12.430
	Nuclear energy	1	12.740
	Energy planning/TA	2	0.287
	Renewable energy	15	4.678
	Forestry/Fuelwood	5	9.204
			74.304

Table 5B continued

	Project Type	No. of Projects	Amount ($US Millions)
Nigeria	Power systems	4	28.594
	Forestry/Fuelwood	4	2.500
			31.094
Senegal	Power systems	3	94.880
	Energy planning/TA	4	3.604
	Renewable energy	17	12.895
	Forestry/Fuelwood	2	1.340
			112.719
Sierra Leone	Energy planning/TA	1	0.0600
	Renewable energy	1	0.0072
			0.0672
Togo	Power systems	4	18.596
	Energy planning/TA	1	0.100
	Renewable energy	1	0.108
			18.804
Upper Volta	Power systems	4	8.980
	Renewable energy	15	5.319
	Forestry/Fuelwood	4	6.800
			21.099

Table 5C.   Latin America and the Caribbean

	Project Type	No. of Projects	Amount ($US Millions)
Argentina	Power systems (generation, transmission, distribution)	9	556.039
	Rural electrification	2	93.000
	Fossil fuels recovery	3	183.000
	Energy planning/ Technical assistance	1	0.890
	Renewable energy	1	0.483
			833.412
Barbados	Fossil fuels recovery	2	1.503
	Energy planning/TA	1	0.034
			1.537
Belize	Power systems	1	1.992

continued

Table 5C continued

	Project Type	No. of Projects	Amount ($US Millions)
Bolivia	Power systems	6	115.437
	Rural electrification	1	69.621
	Fossil fuels recovery	4	89.722
	Nuclear energy	1	0.042
	Energy planning/TA	4	1.815
	Renewable energy	2	0.186
	Forestry/Fuelwood	1	0.130
			276.953
Brazil	Power systems	25	1,446.390
	Rural electrification	1	55.700
	Fossil fuels recovery	2	0.199
	Nuclear energy	2	2.250
	Renewable energy	4	.515
			1,505.054
Chile	Power systems	4	206.700
	Fossil fuels recovery	2	1.953
	Nuclear energy	5	5.361
	Geothermal energy	4	3.693
			217.707
Colombia	Power systems	15	631.296
	Rural electrification	1	7.000
	Fossil fuels recovery	2	0.361
	Energy planning/TA	3	8.630
			647.287
Costa Rica	Power systems	3	151.400
	Rural electrification	2	38.500
	Energy planning/TA	3	1.521
	Renewable energy	1	3.000
	Forestry/Fuelwood	1	0.020
	Geothermal energy	1	4.100
			198.541
Cuba	Nuclear energy	1	0.022
	Renewable energy	1	0.018
			0.040
Dominican Republic			
	Power systems	4	72.8000
	Energy planning/TA	3	3.8102
	Renewable energy	2	0.0003
			76.6105

Table 5C continued

	Project Type	No. of Projects	Amount ($US Millions)
Ecuador	Power systems	11	297.440
	Rural electrification	1	25.000
	Fossil fuels recovery	5	38.230
	Energy planning/TA	3	0.338
			361.008
El Salvador	Power systems	3	118.586
	Energy planning/TA	1	1.000
	Geothermal energy	5	98.482
			218.068
Guatemala	Power systems	6	270.900
	Rural electrification	1	8.000
	Fossil fuels recovery	1	0.238
	Renewable energy	1	0.040
			279.178
Guyana	Power systems	4	13.79
	Forestry/Fuelwood	2	6.00
			19.79
Haiti	Power systems	6	25.180
	Energy planning/TA	3	5.591
	Renewable energy	2	0.757
			31.528
Honduras	Power systems	6	135.96
	Rural electrification	1	10.00
	Geothermal energy	1	0.76
			146.72
Jamaica	Power systems	2	23.300
	Rural electrification	5	29.092
	Fossil fuels recovery	1	- - - - - -
	Energy planning/TA	2	1.263
	Renewable energy	1	0.014
			53.669
Mexico	Rural electrification	3	280.000
	Fossil fuels recovery	3	316.100
	Energy planning/TA	2	0.096
	Renewable energy	5	2.602
	Geothermal energy	1	0.170
			598.968
Montserrat	Renewable energy	1	- - - - - -

continued

Table 5C continued

	Project Type	No. of Projects	Amount ($US Millions)
Nicaragua	Power systems	4	47.489
	Rural electrification	2	16.672
	Renewable energy	1	0.900
	Geothermal energy	2	42.006
			107.067
Panama	Power systems	3	170.000
	Rural electrification	1	0.147
	Energy planning/TA	2	0.300
	Renewable energy	2	0.400
			170.847
Paraguay	Power systems	4	99.860
	Energy planning/TA	2	0.846
	Forestry/Fuelwood	1	0.860
			101.566
Peru	Power systems	8	77.891
	Fossil fuels recovery	1	1.330
	Energy planning/TA	7	9.884
	Renewable energy	6	3.299
	Forestry/Fuelwood	3	1.637
			94.041
St. Lucia/ St. Vincent	Energy planning/TA	1	0.07
	Renewable energy	1	- - - - -
	Geothermal energy	1	1.74
			1.81
Surinam	Power systems	1	1.071
Trinidad and Tobago	Rural electrification	1	0.870
Uruguay	Power systems	3	85.500
	Fossil fuels recovery	1	0.143
			85.643
Venezuela	Energy planning/TA	2	0.051

Table 5D. East Africa

	Project Type	No. of Projects	Amount ($US Millions)
Botswana	Power systems (generation, transmission, distribution)	1	3.900
	Rural electrification	1	1.120
	Fossil fuels recovery	1	0.039
	Energy planning/ Technical assistance	2	3.092
	Renewable energy	2	1.115
			9.266
Burundi	Power systems	13	21.957
	Rural electrification	2	2.196
	Energy planning/TA	3	3.240
	Renewable energy	2	0.024
	Forestry/Fuelwood	3	7.398
			34.815
Comoros	Power systems	1	1.07
	Renewable energy	1	1.27
			2.34
Djibouti	Power systems	1	2.850
	Renewable energy	2	0.120
	Geothermal	2	0.471
			3.441
Ethiopia	Power systems	1	10.700
	Energy planning/TA	1	0.043
	Renewable energy	3	0.266
	Forestry/Fuelwood	2	14.700
	Geothermal	6	8.241
			33.950
Kenya	Power systems	10	200.379
	Rural electrification	3	1.577
	Fossil fuels recovery	1	20.000
	Energy planning/TA	2	2.893
	Renewable energy	8	1.349
	Forestry/Fuelwood	2	20.148
	Geothermal	6	55.024
	Miscellaneous	2	5.443
			306.813
Lesotho	Power systems	1	0.730
	Energy planning/TA	3	2.216
	Renewable energy	3	4.574
			7.520

continued

Table 5D continued

	Project Type	No. of Projects	Amount ($US Millions)
Madagascar	Power systems	10	106.565
	Fossil fuels recovery	1	0.238
	Renewable energy	4	2.140
	Geothermal	1	0.069
			109.012
Malawi	Power systems	10	101.333
	Renewable energy	1	0.135
	Forestry/Fuelwood	1	7.280
			108.748
Mauritius	Power systems	7	35.994
	Renewable energy	2	0.108
	Forestry/Fuelwood	1	2.700
			38.802
Mozambique	Power systems	5	13.822
	Energy planning/TA	1	0.178
			14.000
Rwanda	Power systems	14	89.175
	Rural electrification	1	7.940
	Fossil fuels recovery	3	0.290
	Renewable energy	4	0.593
	Forestry/Fuelwood	1	3.000
			100.998
Somalia	Power systems	1	21.700
	Renewable energy	1	0.155
	Forestry/Fuelwood	1	0.026
			21.881
Sudan	Power systems	3	73.300
	Rural electrification	2	44.300
	Energy planning/TA	2	0.635
	Renewable energy	7	4.043
	Forestry/Fuelwood	1	0.122
			122.400
Swaziland	Energy planning/TA	1	0.092
	Renewable energy	1	0.450
			0.542

Table 5D continued

	Project Type	No. of Projects	Amount ($US Millions)
Tanzania	Power systems	16	150.442
	Rural electrification	1	11.100
	Fossil fuels recovery	3	1.352
	Energy planning/TA	4	3.404
	Renewable energy	8	1.114
	Forestry/Fuelwood	3	30.080
	Geothermal	1	0.020
			197.512
Uganda	Energy planning/TA	2	0.921
Zaire	Power systems	4	55.155
	Fossil fuels recovery	1	4.100
	Energy planning/TA	1	0.209
	Renewable energy	3	0.049
			59.513
Zambia	Power systems	4	160.290
	Fossil fuels recovery	2	6.388
	Energy planning/TA	2	0.183
	Forestry/Fuelwood	1	16.800
			183.661

Table 5E. East Asia and the Pacific

	Project Type	No. of Projects	Amount ($US Millions)
Cambodia	Energy planning/ Technical assistance	1	0.06
China	Energy planning/TA	3	0.71
Fiji	Power systems (generation, transmission, distribution)	6	58.807
	Rural electrification	1	0.017
	Renewable energy	1	- - - - - - -
			58.824
Indonesia	Power systems	40	1,246.591
	Rural electrification	3	66.982
	Fossil fuels recovery	23	118.457
	Energy planning/TA	8	21.432
	Renewable energy	6	2.495
			1,455.957
Korea	Power systems	5	186.800
	Fossil fuels recovery	4	55.547
	Energy planning/TA	3	0.962
	Renewable energy	5	0.655
	Forestry/Fuelwood	1	14.000
			257.964
Laos	Power systems	8	69.791
	Rural electrification	1	0.120
	Energy planning/TA	1	1.400
			71.311
Malaysia	Power systems	15	290.784
	Fossil fuels recovery	1	0.403
	Energy planning/TA	3	1.255
			292.442
Mongolia	Energy planning/TA	1	0.313
New Caledonia	Power systems	7	5.314
	Rural electrification	1	0.800
			6.114
New Hebrides	Power systems	1	0.166
New Zealand	Geothermal energy	1	0.238

Table 5E continued

	Project Type	No. of Projects	Amount ($US Millions)
Papua New Guinea	Power systems	2	11.645
	Energy planning/TA	1	0.113
	Renewable energy	1	2.700
			14.458
Philippines	Power systems	9	239.250
	Rural electrification	2	68.650
	Fossil fuels recovery	5	16.740
	Nuclear energy	2	0.250
	Energy planning/TA	2	2.780
	Renewable energy	5	13.919
	Forestry/Fuelwood	2	2.100
	Geothermal energy	1	2.300
			345.989
Polynesia	Power systems	2	3.497
	Rural electrification	1	6.560
	Renewable energy	1	0.450
			10.507
Seychelles	Renewable enrgy	1	0.049
Taiwan	Power systems	1	0.017
Thailand	Power systems	20	532.259
	Rural electrification	4	42.993
	Fossil fuels recovery	4	79.800
	Energy planning/TA	8	7.901
	Renewable energy	8	6.588
	Geothermal energy	1	- - - - - - -
			669.541
Tonga	Power systems	1	0.190
	Geothermal energy	1	0.007
			0.197
Vietnam	Power systems	2	9.59
	Fossil fuels recovery	2	110.0
			119.59
Western Samoa	Power systems	5	8.017
	Rural electrification	2	0.201
	Renewable energy	1	0.087
			8.305

Table 5F.   South Asia

	Project Type	No. of Projects	Amount ($US Millions)
Bangladesh	Power systems (generation, transmission, distribution)	15	96.573
	Rural electrification	2	56.400
	Fossil fuels recovery	6	30.422
	Nuclear energy	1	0.030
	Energy planning/ Technical assistance	11	15.156
			198.581
Burma	Power systems	8	51.397
	Fossil fuels recovery	6	145.551
	Energy planning/TA	1	0.132
			197.080
India	Power systems	19	903.172
	Rural electrification	2	115.000
	Fossil fuels recovery	18	453.141
	Nuclear energy	3	0.152
	Energy planning/TA	14	10.056
	Renewable energy	11	3.132
	Forestry/Fuelwood	1	3.830
	Geothermal energy	2	1.365
			1,489.848
Nepal	Power systems	16	92.018
	Energy planning/TA	6	6.642
	Renewable energy	8	3.184
	Forestry/Fuelwood	2	0.900
			102.744
Pakistan	Power systems	35	592.409
	Rural electrification	1	0.418
	Fossil fuels recovery	8	165.435
	Nuclear energy	3	1.663
	Energy planning/TA	6	10.770
	Forestry/Fuelwood	2	2.270
			772.965
Sri Lanka	Power systems	9	34.930
	Energy planning/TA	2	1.018
	Renewable energy	5	1.161
	Forestry/Fuelwood	1	0.800
			37.909

Table 5G.   Regional Projects

	Project Type	No. of Projects	Amount ($US Millions)
Europe, Middle East, North Africa	Fossil fuels recovery	1	- - - - - - -
	Nuclear energy	2	1.350
	Energy planning/ Technical assistance	7	2.917
	Renewable energy	2	0.093
			4.360
Africa	Rural electrification	3	0.046
	Nuclear energy	9	0.336
	Energy planning/TA	3	4.683
	Renewable energy	8	1.070
	Forestry/Fuelwood	1	1.607
			7.742
Latin America and the Caribbean	Power systems (generation, transmission, distribution)	2	54.000
	Energy planning/TA	9	3.052
	Renewable energy	4	2.637
			59.689
Asia and the Pacific	Rural electrification	2	0.280
	Fossil fuels recovery	3	0.020
	Energy planning/TA	15	3.537
	Renewable energy	4	0.161
	Geothermal energy	1	0.070
			4.068

Table 5H.   Global Projects

Project Type	No. of Projects	Amount ($US Millions)
Power systems (generation, transmission, distribution)	8	0.222
Rural electrification	1	0.290
Fossil fuels recovery	16	4.792
Nuclear energy	14	7.350
Energy planning/ Technical assistance	42	30.599
Renewable energy	78	46.683
Forestry/Fuelwood	6	27.678
Geothermal energy	2	0.235
		117.849

SOURCE: All energy projects from sources in Table 4.

Bibliography

A SELECT LIST FOR THE GENERAL READER

Books

Blair, John M. *The Control of Oil.* New York: Vintage Books, 1976.

Eckholm, Erik. *Losing Ground: Environmental Stress and World Food Prospects.* New York: Norton, 1976.

Greenwood, Ted; Harold A. Feiveson; and Theodore B. Taylor. *Nuclear Proliferation: Motivations, Capabilities, and Strategies for Control.* New York: McGraw-Hill, 1977.

Hansen, Roger D. *Beyond the North-South Stalemate.* New York: McGraw-Hill, 1979.

The Independent Commission on International Development Issues (popularly referred to as the Brandt Commission). *North—South: A Programme for Survival.* Cambridge, Massachusetts: M.I.T. Press, 1980.

Lovins, Amory B. *Soft Energy Paths: Toward a Durable Peace.* Cambridge, Mass.: Ballinger, 1977.

Odell, Peter R., and Luis Vallenilla. *The Pressures of Oil: A Strategy for Economic Revival.* London: Harper and Row, 1978.

Sampson, Anthony. *The Seven Sisters.* New York: Viking Press, 1975.

U.S. General Accounting Office, Comptroller General. *The United States and International Energy Issues: Report to the Congress.* EMD-78-105. Washington, D.C.: General Accounting Office, December 18, 1978.

Ward, Barbara. *Progress for a Small Planet.* New York: Norton, 1979.

Wilson, Carroll. *COAL: Bridge to the Future* Cambridge, Mass.: Ballinger, 1980.

Articles

Dunn, Lewis A. "Proliferation Watch." *Foreign Policy* (Fall 1979): 71-89.

Healey, Denis. "Oil, Money and Recession." *Foreign Affairs* 58 (Winter 1979/80): 217-30.

Henry, David A. "Energy and Development: Fueling Change." In Jairam Ramesh and Charles Weiss, Jr., eds., *Mobilizing Technology for World Development*, pp. 196-203. New York: Praeger, 1979.

Nye, Joseph S., Jr. "We Tried Harder (And Did More)." *Foreign Policy* (Fall 1979): 101-4.

Quirós Corradi, Alberto. "Energy and the Exercise of Power." *Foreign Affairs* 57 (Summer 1979): 145-66.

Stobaugh, Robert, and Daniel Yergin. "After the Second Shock: Pragmatic Energy Strategies." *Foreign Affairs* 57 (Spring 1979): 836-71.

ADDITIONAL READING AND MATERIAL FOR THE SPECIALIST

Energy and Development: Political and Economic Background

General

Bradman, John R., and Richard E. Hamilton. *A Comparison of Energy Projections to 1985.* International Energy Agency Monograph no. 1. Paris: Organization for Economic Cooperation and Development, January 1979.

Gardner, Richard N. "Nuclear Energy and World Order: Implications for International Organization." Report of Conference at the United Nations and the Institute on Man and Science, May 1976. Rensselaerville, N.Y. (Photocopied.)

Leach, Gerald; Chris Lewis; Frederick Romig; Gerald Foley; and Ariane van Buren. *A Low Energy Strategy for the United Kingdom.* London: International Institute for Environment and Development Science Reviews, 1979.

Schurr, Sam H.; Joel Darmstadter; Harry Perry; William Ramsay; and Milton Russell. *Energy in America's Future: The Choices Before Us.* Baltimore: RFF-Johns Hopkins University Press, 1979.

Taylor, Vince. "Energy: the Easy Path." *Not Man Apart* 9 (June 1979): 6-8.

Developing Countries

Attiga, Ali Ahmed. "Global Energy Transition and the Third World. *Third World Quarterly* 1 (October 1979): 39-56.

Dunn, Robert M., Jr. "The Less Developed Countries." In Joseph A. Yager and Eleanor B. Steinberg, eds., *Energy and U.S. Foreign Policy*, pp. 163-81. Cambridge, Mass.: Ballinger, 1974.

Fishlow, Albert; Richard S. Weinert; Marina von N. Whitman; Kenneth B. Lipper; and Helen B. Junz. "The Third World: Public Debt, Private Profit." *Foreign Policy* (Spring 1978): 132-69.

Howe, James W., and staff of Overseas Development Council. *U.S. Energy Policy in the Non-OPEC Third World.* Washington, D.C.: ODC, 1979.

International Consultative Group on Nuclear Energy. *Nuclear Energy and International Cooperation: A Third World View of the Erosion of Confidence.* New York: The Rockefeller Foundation, 1979.

Mazrui, Ali A. *The Barrel of the Gun and the Barrel of Oil in the North-South Equation.* New York: Institute for World Order, 1978.

World Bank. *World Development Report 1979.* Washington, D.C.: World Bank, 1979.

OPEC

Levy, Walter J. "The Years that the Locust Hath Eaten: Oil Policy and OPEC Development Prospects." *Foreign Affairs* 57 (Winter 1978/79): 287-305.

"Oil: Why the Saudis Offer No Solution." *Business Week*, June 8, 1979, pp. 110-15.

"OPEC: The Cartel's Deadly New Sting." *Newsweek*, April 9, 1979, pp. 96-104.

Energy Use in Developing Countries

Bonn International Conference Energy Resources Working Group. "Agricultural Production: Research and Development Strategies for the 1980s." Conference document, 1979. (Mimeo.)

Cecelski, Elizabeth; Joy Dunkerley; and William Ramsay. *Household Energy and the Poor in the Third World.* Washington, D.C.: Resources for the Future, 1979.

Chauhan, Sumi. *A Village in a Million—An Energy Portrait of Akbarpur-Barota, India.* London: Earthscan–International Institute for Environment and Development, 1979.

Dunkerley, Joy, ed. *International Comparisons of Energy Consumption.* Washington, D.C.: Resources for the Future, 1978.

Earthscan. *Energy for the Third World.* Press-briefing document. London: Earthscan–International Institute for Environment and Development, 1978.

Floor, W.M. "Energy Options in Rural Areas of the Third World." Paper for Eighth World Forestry Congress, Jakarta, Indonesia, October 1978.

Floor, W.M. "The Energy Sector of the Sahelian Countries." Paper for Second Conference of the Club du Sahel, Ottawa, Canada, May 1977.

Goldemberg, José. "Consumption Energy Patterns in the United States and Latin American Countries." Paper for Center for Environmental Studies, Princeton University, Princeton, New Jersey. (Unpublished.)

Gordian Associates, Inc. "LDC Energy Supply/Demand Balance and Financing Requirements." Report for U.S. Department of Energy Office of International Affairs, February 27, 1978.

Howe, James W., and staff of the Overseas Development Council. "Energy for the Villages of Africa." Paper for U.S. Agency for International Development, February 25, 1977.

Howe, James W.; James J. Tarrant; and Julie A. Martin. "South-North

Cooperation on Energy for Development." Paper for Cairo Workshop on Energy Futures for Developing Countries, November 20, 1978.

Palmedo, Philip F.; Robert Nathans; Edward Beardsworth; and Samuel Hale, Jr. *Energy Needs, Uses and Resources in Developing Countries.* Upton, N.Y.: Brookhaven National Laboratory, 1978.

Parikh, Jyoti, and Kirit Parikh. "Energy Requirements—Approaches to Projection." Paper for meeting of World Energy Study from a Southern Perspective, Institute of Physics, São Paulo, Brazil, November 1978.

Energy Resources in Developing Countries

General
Baum, Vladimir. "Energy in Developing Countries: Prospects and Problems." In *Nuclear Power and Its Fuel Cycle.* IAEA-CN-36/581, vol. 1. Vienna: International Atomic Energy Agency, 1977.

Brown, Norman L., ed. *Renewable Energy Resources and Rural Application in the Developing World.* Boulder, Colorado: Westview Press, 1978.

International Energy Agency. *Workshop on Energy Data of Developing Countries,* vols. 1 and 2. Paris: Organization for Economic Cooperation and Development, 1979.

Martin, Jean-Marie. "Energy: Re-evaluation of Needs and Re-orientation of Technology." Paper for Symposium on Science and Technology in Development Planning, Mexico City, May 28–June 1, 1979. (Offset.)

Pendse, D.R. "The Energy Crisis and Third World Options." *Third World Quarterly* 1 (October 1979): 69-88.

Reddy, Amulya Kumar N. "Energy Options for the Third World." *Bulletin of the Atomic Scientists* (May 1978): 28-33.

SEMA. *New Energy for Development: Evaluation of New Energy Sources for Developing Countries.* Paris: République francaise, Ministère de la Coopération, 1978.

United Kingdom. Atomic Energy Research Establishment, Energy Technology Support Unit. "Renewable Energy Sources for Developing Countries—An Initial Appraisal." Paper for U.K. Ministry of Overseas Development, September 1978.

United Nations Conference on Trade and Development. *Energy Supplies for Developing Countries: Issues in Transfer and Development of Technology.* TD/B/C.6/31. Geneva: United Nations, 1978.

U.S. Department of Energy, with representatives of the government of Egypt. *Joint Egypt/United States Report on Egypt/United States Cooperative Energy Assessment.* DOE/1A-0002/01-05, vols. 1-5. Washington, D.C,: DOE, April 1979.

Conventional (Electricity and Fossil Fuels)
Gray, John E.; Myron B. Kratzer; Karen E. Leslie; Hilliard W. Paige; and Steven B. Shantzis. *International Cooperation on Breeder Reactors.* New York: The Rockefeller Foundation, 1978.

Grossling, Bernardo F. "A Long-Range Outlook of World Petroleum Prospects." Paper for Subcommittee on Energy of the Joint Economic Committee, Congress of the United States, March 2, 1978. (Photocopied.)

Grossling, Bernardo F. "The Petroleum Exploration Challenge with Respect to the Developing Nations." In R. Meyer, ed., *The Future Supply of Nature-Made Petroleum and Gas*, pp. 57-69. New York: Pergamon Press, 1977.

Grossling, Bernardo F. "Petroleum Exploration in Developing Countries and Considerations about Its Financing." *Natural Resources Forum 3* (April 1979): 299-307.

Sabato, Jorge A., and Jairam Ramesh. "Nuclear Energy Programs in the Developing World: Their Rationale and Impacts." Paper presented to Royal Institution Forum on Energy Strategies for the Third World, London, June 20-21, 1979. (Photocopied.)

Tanger, Michael. "Oil Exploration Strategies for Developing Countries." *Natural Resources Forum 2* (July 1978): 319-26.

Turvey, Ralph, and Dennis Anderson. *Electricity Economics.* Baltimore: Johns Hopkins, 1977.

U.S. Department of Energy. *The 1985 Oil Production of 21 Oil-Producing Non-OPEC Countries.* DOE/1A-0007. Washington, D.C.: DOE, March 1979.

U.S. Department of Energy, and U.S. Geological Survey. *Report on the Petroleum Resources of the Federal Republic of Nigeria.* DOE/1A-0008. Washington, D.C.: DOE and U.S. Geological Survey, October 1979.

U.S. General Accounting Office. *Issues Related to Foreign Oil Supply Diversification.* ID-79-36. Washington, D.C.: GAO, May 31, 1979.

World Bank. *A Program to Accelerate Petroleum Production in the Developing Countries.* Washington, D.C.: World Bank, 1979.

World Bank. *Coal Development Potential and Prospects in the Developing Countries.* Washington, D.C.: World Bank, 1979.

World Bank. *Energy and Petroleum in Non-OPEC Developing Countries, 1974-80.* Washington, D.C.: World Bank, February 1976.

World Bank. *Rural Electrification Sector Paper.* Washington, D.C.: World Bank, 1975.

Traditional (Firewood and Charcoal)

Arnold, J.E.M. "Wood Energy and Rural Communities." *Natural Resources Forum 3* (April 1979): 229-49.

Eckholm, Erik P. *Planting for the Future: Forestry for Human Needs.* Worldwatch Paper 26. Washington, D.C.: Worldwatch Institute, February 1979.

Evans, Ianto. "Using Firewood More Efficiently." Paper for Eighth World Forestry Congress, Jakarta, Indonesia, October 1978. (Photocopied.)

Freeman, Peter H. "Forestry in Development Assistance." Report to U.S. Agency for International Development, September 1979. (Offset.)

French, David. "Firewood in Africa." Prepared for the Africa Bureau Firewood Workshop, U.S. Agency for International Development, June 12-14, 1978, Washington, D.C. (Photocopied.)

Goldemberg, J., and R.I. Brown. "Cooking Stoves: the State of the Art." University of São Paulo, São Paulo, Brazil, 1979. (Mimeo.)

Spears, John S. "Wood as an Energy Source: The Situation in the Developing World." Paper presented to 103rd Annual Meeting of the American Forestry Association, October 8, 1978. (Photocopied.)

World Bank. *Prospects for Traditional and Non-Conventional Energy Sources in Developing Countries.* Washington, D.C.: World Bank, July 1979.

"New" Renewable (Solar Wind, biomass, mini-hydro)

Agarwal, Anil. *Whose Solar Power?* Earthscan Press Briefing Document no. 19. London: Earthscan, 1979.

Barnett, Andrew; Leo Pyle; and S.K. Subramanian. *Biogas Technology in the Third World: A Multidisciplinary Review.* Ottawa: International Development Research Centre, 1978.

Brown, Norman L. "Testimony before the Subcommittee on Domestic and International Scientific Planning, Analysis and Cooperation of the Committee on Science and Technology," U.S. House of Representatives, July 26, 1978. (Mimeo.)

Brown, Norman L., and James W. Howe. "Solar Energy for Village Development." *Science* 199 (February 1978): 652.

Commission of the European Communities. *Solar Energy for Development,* proceedings of the International Conference held at Varese, Italy, March 26–29, 1979. The Hague: Martinus Nijhoff, 1979.

Desai, B.G. "Solar Electrification and Rural Electrification—A Techno-Economic Review." In F. de Winter and M. Cox, eds., *Sun—Mankind's Future Source of Energy,* vol. 1, pp. 211-13. New York: Pergamon Press, 1978.

French, David. "The Economics of Renewable Energy Systems for Developing Countries." Washington, D.C.: January 1979. (Offset.)

Hammer, Turi. "Report from African Solar Energy Workshop, 21st-26th May 1979, Atlanta, Georgia, USA." Bergen, Norway: Chr. Michelsen Institute, 1979. (Offset.)

National Academy of Sciences. *Energy for Rural Development.* Washington, D.C.: NAS, 1976.

National Academy of Sciences. *Methane Generation from Human, Animal and Agricultural Wastes.* Washington, D.C.: NAS, 1977.

Parikh, Jyoti K. "Assessment of Solar Applicators for Transfer of Technology—A Case of Solar Pump." *Solar Energy* 21:99-106.

Paulissen, L.M. and J.C. van Doorn. "L'Energie Eolienne dans le Sahel." Paper for Second Conference of the Club du Sahel, Ottawa, Canada, May 1977.

Peters, Wendy. "Photovoltaic Cells to Generate Villages' Power under Saudi/U.S. Agreement." *Canadian Renewable Energy News,* May 1979, p. 10.

Rosenblum, Louis; William J. Bifano; Gerald Hein; and Anthony F. Ratajcizak. *Photovoltaic Power Systems for Rural Areas of Developing Countries.* National Aeronautics and Space Administration Technical Memorandum 79097. Cleveland, Ohio: NASA Lewis Research Center, 1979.

Smil, Vaclav. "Intermediate Technology in China." *Bulletin of the Atomic Scientists* 33 (March 1977): 25-31.

Tanzanian National Scientific Research Council. *Workshop on Solar Energy for the Villages of Tanzania.* Dar es Salaam, Tanzania: TNSRC, 1978.

United Nations Environment Programme. *Solar-2000.* UNEP Report 8. Nairobi: United Nations, March 1979.

United Nations Industrial Development Organization. *Technology for Solar Energy Utilization.* Development and Transfer of Technology Series no. 5. New York: United Nations, 1978.

U.S. Congress. Office of Technology Assessment. *Applications of Solar Technology to Today's Energy Needs,* vol. I. Washington, D.C.: OTA, June 1978.

Walton, J.D., Jr.; A.H. Roy; and S.H. Bomar, Jr. *A State of the Art Survey of Solar Powered Irrigation Pumps, Solar Cookers, and Wood Burning Stoves for Use in Sub-Sahara Africa.* Atlanta, Georgia: Georgia Institute of Technology, 1978.

Institutional Responses: North and South

Aid Donors (including OPEC)

Ashworth, John H. *Renewable Energy Sources for the World's Poor: A Review of Current International Development Assistance Programs.* SERI/TR-51-195. Golden, Colorado: Solar Energy Research Institute for the U.S. Department of Energy, October 1979.

Ashworth, John H. "Technology Diffusion Through Foreign Assistance: Making Renewable Energy Sources Available to the World's Poor." Golden, Colorado: Solar Energy Research Institute, 1979. (Offset.)

Commission of the European Communities. "A New Cooperation Contract (Second Lomé Convention)." Information Memo. Brussels: EEC, October 1979.

Commission of the European Communities. "Aspects of External Measures by the Community in the Energy Sector." Communication from the Commission to the Council, Brussels, February 6, 1979. (Offset.)

Commission of the European Communities. "Cooperation with Developing Countries in the Field of Energy." Communication from the Commission to the Council, Brussels, July 31, 1978. (Offset).

Commission of the European Communities. "Instruments of Mining and Energy Cooperation with the ACP Countries." Communication from the Commission to the Council, Strasbourg, March 14, 1979. (Offset).

Commission of the European Communities. "Report from the Commission to the Council Concerning Cooperation with Developing Countries in the Field of Energy." Document 74/79. Brussels, April 23, 1979.

Commission of the European Communities. "Solar Energy: A New Area of ACP-EEC Cooperation." In *Europe Information Series.* Brussels: European Economic Community, 1979.

Congressional Research Service, Library of Congress. *Reader on Nuclear Nonproliferation.* Prepared for the Subcommittee on Energy, Nuclear Proliferation and Federal Services of the Committee on Governmental Affairs, U.S. Senate, 95th Cong., 2d sess., Washington, D.C.: Government Printing Office, December 1978.

"Energy in the ACP States." *The Courier*, September–October 1978, pp. 64–99.

Federal Republic of Germany. Ministry for Research and Technology. *Energy Research and Energy Technologies Program, 1977–1980.* Bonn: Federal Ministry for Research and Technology, 1977.

Hoffmann, Thomas, and Brian Johnson. "Bypassing Oil and the Atom: The Politics of Aid and World Energy." *Energy Policy* 7 (June 1979): 90–101.

Organization for Economic Cooperation and Development. *Development Cooperation: Efforts and Policies of the Members of the Development Assistance Committee.* Paris: OECD, November 1978.

Organization for Economic Cooperation and Development. *1978 OECD Development Cooperation Review.* Paris: OECD, 1978.

Organization for Economic Cooperation and Development. "Report by the Working Party of the Council to Develop a Co-ordinated Effort to Help Developing Countries Bring into Use Technologies Related to Renewable Energy." Paris, May 7, 1979. (Mimeo.)

Palmedo, Philip F.; Robert Nathans; Edward Beardsworth; and Gerhard Tschannerl. *Programmatic Areas for U.S. Assistance for Energy in the Developing Countries.* Upton, New York: Policy Analysis Division, Brookhaven National Laboratory, December 1978.

Shihata, Ibrahim. *OPEC Aid, the OPEC Fund and Cooperation with Commercial Sources of Development Finance.* Vienna: OPEC Special Fund, 1978.

Shihata, Ibrahim. "The OPEC Special Fund and the North-South Dialogue." *Third World Quarterly* 1 (October 1979): 28–38.

Shihata, Ibrahim, and Robert Mabro. *The OPEC Aid Record.* Vienna: OPEC Special Fund, January 1978.

Tanner, James. "OPEC Members Agree They Should Give More Financial Aid to Developing States." *Wall Street Journal*, December 19, 1979, p. 21.

Ulinski, Carol A. "Fuelwood and Other Renewable Energies in Africa: A Brief Summary of U.S.-Supported Programs." Background paper for the Workshop on Fuelwood and Other Renewable Fuels in Africa, Paris, November 29–30, 1979. (Photocopied.)

United Nations. Conference on Trade and Development. *Financial Solidarity for Development—Efforts and Institutions of the Members of OPEC.* TD/B/627. New York: United Nations, 1977.

U.S. Congress. House. Committee on Foreign Affairs. *International Development Cooperation Act of 1979. Report to Accompany H.R. 3324*, 96th Cong., 1st sess., 1979, H. Rept. 96-79, pp. 7–9, 40–41.

U.S. Congress. House. Committee on International Relations. *Nuclear Non-Proliferation Act of 1977. Report to Accompany H.R. 8638*, 95th Cong., 1st sess., 1977, H. Rept. 95-587.

U.S. Congress. Office of Technology Assessment. *Nuclear Proliferation and Safeguards.* New York: Praeger, 1977.

U.S. Congress. Senate. Committee on Governmental Affairs, Committee on Energy and Natural Resources, and Committee on Foreign Relations. *Nuclear Non-Proliferation Act of 1977. Report to Accompany S. 897*, 95th Cong., 1st sess., 1977, S. Rept. 95-467.

U.S. Department of Energy. *Domestic Policy Review of Solar Energy: Final Report, International Panel.* TID-28830/2. Washington, D.C.: DOE, October 1978.

U.S. Department of Energy. *Domestic Policy Review of Solar Energy: vol. I., International Panel Technical Cooperation Sub-Panel Report.* TID-28830/1. Washington, D.C.: DOE, August 22, 1978.

Vance, Cyrus. Address to the 33rd session of the United Nations General Assembly, New York, September 29, 1978.

International Institutions and the U.N. System

Boskey, Shirley. Statement to the U.N. Conference on Science and Technology for Development. International Relations Department, World Bank, August 27, 1979.

Byer, Trevor A., "The End of the Paris Energy Dialogue and the Need for an International Energy Institute." *Energy Policy* 6 (December 1978): 254-76.

Friedmann, Efrain. "Energy Activities of the World Bank." *Natural Resources Forum* 3 (October 1978): 91-94.

Hoffmann, Thomas. "Fuel for the Fire—the Reappraisal of Multilateral Energy Aid." *Energy Policy* 6 (December 1978): 332-38.

Johnson, Brian. *Whose Power to Choose?* Washington, D.C.: International Institute for Environment and Development, 1977.

North-South Institute. *Third World Deficits and the "Debt Crisis."* Ottawa: The North-South Institute, 1977.

Stein, Robert E., and Brian Johnson. *Banking on the Biosphere?* Lexington, Mass.: Lexington Books, 1979.

United Nations Economic and Social Council. *Cross-Organisational Analysis of the Energy Programmes of the United Nations Systems.* Secretary-General, Official Report. E/AC.51/99, April 23, 1979, and Addendum E/AC.51/99 Add. 1, April 30, 1979.

United Nations Economic and Social Council. *Strengthening International Co-operation in Energy: Possible Approaches.* Secretary-General, Official Report: E/C.7/75, April 11, 1977.

United Nations Environment Programme. *Survey of Activities Related to the Implementation of the Objectives of Selected Areas of the Environment Programme: Energy.* UNEP Report no. 5 (1979). Nairobi: United Nations, 1979.

United Nations General Assembly. Intergovernmental Group of Experts on Mineral and Energy Exploration in Developing Countries. *Development and International Co-operation: Multilateral Development Assistance for the Exploration of Natural Resources,* 33d sess., August 1978.

United Nations General Assembly. *Resolution 33/148: Calling for a 1981 Conference on New and Renewable Sources of Energy.* New York: United Nations, December 20, 1978.

United Nations General Assembly. *Resolution 34/190: Calling for a 1981 Conference on New and Renewable Sources of Energy.* New York: United Nations, December 18, 1979.

World Bank. *World Debt Tables*, vols. 1 and 2. Washington, D.C.: World Bank, October 20, 1978.

Developing Country Governments
Byer, Trevor A. "Jamaica—A Case Study of Energy Planning." *Natural Resources Forum* 3 (January 1979): 117-32.

Kral, Pavel. "Energy Planning in Developing Countries." *Natural Resources Forum* 3 (1978): 379-83.

Lopez Portillo, José. Address to the 34th session of the United Nations General Assembly, New York, September 27, 1979.

Miller, Judith. "In Poor Lands, Oil Price Increases Shock Economies and Erode Hope." *The New York Times*, July 4, 1979, A1.

Nossiter, Bernard. "Poorer Countries Persuade OPEC to Negotiate Oil Prices and Supply." *The New York Times*, September 18, 1979, A1.

Nossiter, Bernard. "Poor Nations Drop Oil-Price Proposal." *The New York Times*, November 19, 1979, A16.

OLADE (Latin American Energy Organization). *Lima Agreement Establishing the Latin American Energy Organization*. Lima, Peru: OLADE, November 1973.

United Nations Conference on Trade and Development. UNCTAD Secretariat. *The Flow of Financial Resources: Investment by Developing Countries in the Energy Sector: A Preliminary Analysis of Long-Term Financing Requirements*. TD/B/C.3/146, September 15, 1978.

United Nations. *Research in Non-Conventional Sources of Energy: Report of the Secretary-General*. Secretary-General, January 1978, annex.

Workshop on Energy Problems of LDCs. "Final Report of Workshop on Energy Problems of LDCs: A Southern Perspective." Submitted to Workshop held in São Paulo, Brazil, December 1978, (offset).

Private Investment

Petroleum
Norway. Ministry of Foreign Affairs. "The Norwegian Petroleum Experience." Annex to the Norwegian National Report to the U.N. Conference on Science and Technology for Development, Vienna, 1979.

U.S. Congress. Senate Committee on Foreign Relations. Subcommittee on Multinational Corporations. *Multinational Oil Corporations and U.S. Foreign Policy: Report Together with Individual Views*, 93rd Cong., 1st and 2d sess., January 2, 1973.

Solar Energy
Agarwal, Anil. "Western Monopoly on Solar Energy." *New Scientist*, October 18, 1979, pp. 175-77.

Cavard, Denise, and Patrick Criqui. "La Stratégie des Pays Industrialisés en Matière de Développement de L'Energie Solaire: Etude Comparée Etats Unis–France." Paper for Conférence de l'Energie Nucléaire aux Nouvelles Sources d'Energie: Vers un Nouvel Ordre Energétique International at CREDIMI, Dijon, France, March 1979. (Mimeo.)

Hein, Gerald F., and Toufig A. Siddiqi. "Utilization of Solar Energy in Developing Countries: Identifying Some Potential Markets." Paper for the U.S. Department of Energy, 1978.

Hoffman, H.K. *Alternative Energy Technologies and Third World Rural Energy Needs: A Case of Emerging Technological Dependency.* Sussex, England: University of Sussex, October 1978.

Keiser, J.T. Address to DOE/Solar Export Opportunities Workshop, Atlanta, Georgia, January 10, 1979. Waltham, Mass.: Thermo Electron Corp. (Offset.)

Passmore, Jeff. "Politics, Technology Dominate Atlanta Solar Convention." *Canadian Renewable Energy News,* June/July 1979, p. 5.

Rosenblum, Louis; William J. Bifano; Larry R. Scudder; William A. Poley; and James P. Cusick. "Photovoltaic Water Pumping Applications: Assessment of the Near-Term Market." Paper for U.S. Department of Energy, March 1978.

U.S. Department of Energy. *Export Potential for Photovoltaic Systems: Preliminary Report.* Washington, D.C.: DOE, April 1979.

U.S. Department of Energy. *Solar Energy Commercialization for African Countries.* HCP/CS/2522. Washington, D.C.: DOE, December 1978.

U.S. Department of Energy. *Solar Energy Commercialization for European Countries.* HCP/CS-4121 and HCP/CS-4250, vols. 1 and 2. Washington, D.C.; DOE, December 1978.

U.S. Department of Energy. *Solar Energy Commercialization for Middle East Countries.* HCP/CS-4192-2. Washington, D.C.: DOE, December 1978.

Index

About the Authors

Thomas Hoffmann, the Acting Director of the International Institute for Environment and Development (IIED, Washington Office), is an international lawyer specializing in energy and development and has recently testified before Congress on international energy issues. He is the author of "Fuel for the Fire: the Reappraisal of Multi-lateral Energy Aid" (*Energy Policy*, December 1978) and, with Brian Johnson, "Bypassing Oil and the Atom: The Politics of Aid and World Energy" (*Energy Policy*, June 1979). He is an Executive Director of the International Development Conference and holds law degrees from the University of Oxford and New York University, where he was a Root-Tilden Scholar.

Brian Johnson writes and lectures extensively on environmental and developmental issues, both in Europe and in the United States. He is the former director of the Ecological Foundation, London, and of the Institute for the Study of International Organization at the University of Sussex, United Kingdom. He has held fellowships at Columbia University and Sussex University and is currently a senior fellow of IIED (London Office). His books include *The Politics of Money* (McGraw-Hill, 1970); *Third World and Environmental Interests in the Law of the Sea* (IIED, 1974); *Whose Power to Choose? International Institutions and the Control of Nuclear Energy* (IIED, 1977); and *Banking on the Biosphere?*, with Robert E. Stein (Lexington Books, 1979).